EDITOR: LEE JOHNS

 MEN-AT-ARMS

THE RUSSO-TURKISH WAR 1877

Text by
IAN DRURY
Colour plates by
RAFFAELE RUGGERI

First published in Great Britain in 1994 by
Osprey, an imprint of Reed Consumer Books Ltd.
Michelin House, 81 Fulham Road,
London SW3 6RB
and Auckland, Melbourne, Singapore and
Toronto

ISBN 1 85532 371 0

Filmset in Great Britain by Keyspools Ltd
Printed through Bookbuilders Ltd, Hong Kong

For a catalogue of all books published by Osprey Military
please write to:

The Marketing Manager,
Consumer Catalogue Department,
Osprey Publishing Ltd,
Michelin House, 81 Fulham Road,
London SW3 6RB

Author's dedication
To Dee – thanks for being a 'Word Processor Widow'
once again.

Acknowledgements
I would like to thank Herbert Woodend and the staff at
the MoD Pattern Room, for their expert assistance.
Thanks also to Dave Hendley, for photography; to
Adrian Whiting for happy afternoons with a Martini-
Henry and a bruised shoulder; and to Richard Brooks,
for introducing me to this Balkan bloodbath in the first
place. Any errors or omissions in this book are, of
course, entirely down to me.

Note on spelling
I have used the spellings employed by 19th- and early
20th-century journalists and historians: thus, e.g.
Adrianopolis rather than Edirne, Philipopolis not
Plovdiv, Russian and Turkish names are rendered as
they appear in contemporary sources.

Publisher's note
Readers may wish to study this title in conjunction with
the following Osprey publications:
MAA 140 *Armies of the Ottoman Turks 1300–1774*
MAA 241 *Russian Army of the Crimean War*

Artist's note
Readers may care to note that the original paintings
from which the colour plates in this book were prepared
are available for private sale. All reproduction copy-
right whatsoever is retained by the publisher. All
enquiries should be addressed to:
Raffaele Ruggeri
Via P. Gubellini, 12
40141 Bologna
Italy
The publishers regret that they can enter into no
correspondence upon this matter.

THE SEEDS OF WAR

On 24 April 1877 Tsar Nicholas II declared war on the Ottoman Empire. It was Russia's fifth war against Turkey in the 19th century, but probably the first to enjoy a measure of popular support, thanks to the growth of Slavic nationalism. The Pan-Slavic-movement exerted a growing influence on Russian policy, helping to propel the country into war despite official opposition from the Ministries of Finance and Foreign Affairs.

Pan-Slavism was a potent cocktail of emotions including commitment to the racial solidarity of Slavic peoples and to the Orthodox Church, and a yearning for liberation from Muslim rule. It gathered force during the 19th century as Balkan society began at last to evolve. Previously, the sheer effort of subsistence farming in south-eastern Europe, as much as Turkish repression, had kept the Christian peasantry firmly under the control of their Muslim landlords. However, as Bosnian Serbs began herding and trading cattle between the European provinces of the Ottoman Empire, a new and prosperous merchant class emerged, upsetting the centuries-old division between Muslim overlords and their subject peoples. The traders' children learned to read; and by the mid-19th century an educated 'middle class' was leading local opposition to continued Turkish rule. The Ottoman regime was never flexible or imaginative enough to accommodate social and economic change in the region. Sporadic risings, repressed with medieval savagery, stoked the fires of Romanian, Bulgarian and Serbian folk memory.

The Russian government attempted to exploit Slavic sentiment for its own ends, promoting the Tsar as the natural leader of all Slavic peoples. Attempts to weld a Slavic union backfired in central Europe: Poland rebelled in 1863 and had to be subdued by the Russian army; the Czechs refused to adopt the Cyrillic alphabet or the Orthodox faith, and

The Russo-Turkish War was the first major conflict for the Tsarist army after Alexander II's abolition of serfdom and the creation of a German-style military reserve system. Although the direction of the campaign in Bulgaria remained nominally in the hands of his brother Grand Duke Nicholas, the Tsar's arrival in July exerted a paralysing influence over Russian strategy. (Author's Collection)

detached themselves from the movement in the late 1860s. In the Balkans, however, Russian leadership was unchallenged. When Slavic peasants in Bosnia-Herzogovina revolted against Turkish rule in 1875 Russian volunteers flocked to join the Serbian army, anticipating a war of liberation.

Serbia and Montenegro declared war on Turkey in 1876, but despite the leadership of the ex-Russian General Cherniaev they were defeated. A rising by Bulgarian Christians, timed to coincide with the Serbian offensive, was brutally suppressed by Ottoman irregulars: modern estimates place civilian casualties at around 30,000 men, women and children. To the Turks the systematic massacre of rebellious peoples was simply a traditional instrument of Ottoman rule, but it stunned Europe as never before.

Sultan Abdul Hamid II came to the throne in 1876 after his insane brother was deposed by a cabal of senior officials. The son of Abdulmecid I and a Circassian dancing girl from the Trebizond slave market, he spent his whole life in fear of assassination – even suppressing the news of Tsar Alexander's murder in 1881. Abdul Hamid II managed to resist pressure for reform until he was overthrown by the 'Young Turks' in 1909. (Author's Collection)

Tales of bestial cruelty flashed across the continent by telegraph, and needed little elaboration to make sensational headlines. In a striking parallel with the 1990s, obscure Balkan provinces suddenly became household names. Russia began mobilization in November 1876, while at the same time advocating a conference of the great powers to create and safeguard Christian provinces in the Turkish-controlled Balkans – foreshadowing the 'safe havens' touted as a solution to another Balkan war in 1993.

In Britain, Gladstone's energetic campaign publicising the 'Balkan horrors' prevented the Conservative government coming to the aid of Turkey; the long-standing British policy of preventing Russia from taking Constantinople was frustrated by public opinion. The London Protocol, issued in March 1877, called upon the Turks to introduce reforms and demobilize. The Sultan refused, recognising that a

Russian invasion was all but inevitable. Since the Turkish army had enjoyed considerable success on the Balkan front during the Crimean War, and most reservists had been called up for the fighting in 1875–6, the Sultan had a battle-hardened army ready for war.

The Russian Plan of Campaign

Nine major wars in the previous two centuries had left Turkey's European provinces heavily fortified. The Russo-Turkish wars of 1788–91, 1806–7, and 1810–11 had all turned on sieges of Turkish fortresses between the lower Danube and the Balkan mountains. In 1774 and 1829 Russian armies had succeeded in breaking through the Turks' defences and arriving outside Constantinople to dictate peace terms; but on both occasions the armies had been all but wiped out by cholera, typhoid and other diseases in the process. The Russian plan of operations for 1877 was designed to repeat General I. Diebitsch's 1829 victory, but without exposing the troops to a Balkan winter.

In earlier campaigns the Russian army had benefited from naval supremacy; the destruction of the Turkish fleet at Chesma in 1770 and again at Navarino in 1827 had enabled the Russians to conduct amphibious operations and supply their forces by sea. However, the Russian Black Sea fleet had been scuttled in Sevastopol during the Crimean War, and the 1856 Treaty of Paris restricted Russian naval forces in the Black Sea to half a dozen small warships. Although Tsar Alexander II repudiated this part of the Treaty in 1871, Russia had built no warships capable of challenging Turkey's squadron of modern ironclads.

The Russian plan was to mobilize 250,000 men and pass through neutral Romania, crossing the Danube upstream of the Turkish fortresses of the Quadrilateral. Leaving detachments to protect its flanks, the main force would advance over the Balkan mountains to Adrianople before marching directly on the Turkish capital. It was hoped that a diversionary offensive in the Caucasus would prevent the Ottomans reinforcing their European armies with troops from Asia Minor. A swift victory was essential: prolonged fighting would inevitably lead to interference by other great powers, and in any case Russia's precarious finances could not sustain a long war.

In 1877 the Turks enjoyed control of the Black Sea, as Sevastopol still lay in ruins with the Russian Black Sea Fleet at the bottom of the harbour. On 14 May four Turkish ironclads shelled Soukoum Kaleh on the Caucasian coast, and landed troops which defeated the garrison and raised the Muslim population in revolt. (Author's Collection)

Russian Forces

In April 1877 the Russian Army of the South comprised four corps, each consisting of two infantry divisions and a cavalry division, plus 96 field guns and 12 horse guns:

VIII Corps (Lt. Gen. Radetzky)

IX Corps (Lt. Gen. Baron Krüdener)

XI Corps (Lt. Gen. Prince Shakofskoi)

XII Corps (Lt. Gen. Vannofsky)

3rd Rifle Brigade (Maj. Gen. Dobrovolsk): four battalions

4th Rifle Brigade (Maj. Gen. Zviazinksi): four battalions

Cossack Division (Lt. Gen. Skoboleff): 20 squadrons and six guns

Unattached Don Cossacks: 54 squadrons and 46 guns

On 6 May the following troops were added and sent to the front by rail:

XIV Corps (Lt. Gen. Zimmerman)

IV Corps (Lt. Gen. Zotof)

XIII Corps (Lt. Gen. Hahn)

Turkish Forces in Europe

The Russians believed that the Turks had about 160,000 troops in Europe: 60,000 in the Danube fortress at Vidin, and 100,000 at Rushchuk, Silistria, Varna and Shumla. Unfortunately for them, this was an underestimate: while few studies of the war agree on the exact number of Turkish troops or their initial deployment, the lowest estimate is 186,000, and most 19th-century histories settle for over 250,000. F. Maurice's 1905 study of the campaign gives the Turkish order of battle as follows:

Vidin: 30,000 under Osman Pasha – 50 infantry battalions, 10 cavalry squadrons and 15 batteries of artillery.

Along the Upper Danube between Rahova, Nikopolis and Sistova: 15,000 – 15 battalions, 4 squadrons and 5 batteries.

Rushchuk and Sistova: 12,000 under Kaisserli Achmed Pasha – 20 battalions, 5 squadrons and 2 batteries.

Silistria: 9,000 under Sulami Pasha – 12 battalions, 3 squadrons and 3 batteries.

Shumla and Eski Dzuma: 55,000 under Achmed Eyoub Pasha – 65 battalions, 30 squadrons (mostly irregular) and 15 batteries.

Varna: 8,000 under Rechid Pasha – 12 battalions, 2 squadrons and 2 batteries.

Sophia, Tirnova, Adrianople and Constantinople were defended by approximately 25,000 men – 45 battalions, 12 squadrons and 8 batteries.

Outside the immediate area of operations the Turks had one major army under Suleiman Pasha in Bosnia-Herzogovina, where it had just extinguished the last flickers of resistance. There were 15,000 troops in Bosnia itself; another 20,000 stationed in Albania – where some of the Ottomans' toughest infantry were recruited, and another 10,000 garri-

THE CAMPAIGNS

One of several European officers serving in the Turkish ranks, Charles Augustus Hobart was an ex-Royal Navy captain who achieved the rank of Pasha. He commanded Turkish naval forces in the Black Sea. (Author's Collection)

soned Novi Bazar. On Crete (the scene of a major rebellion in the 1860s) and in European Turkey there were about 45,000 more troops ready to hand.

These figures are probably nearer the truth than the contemporary Russian estimates, but they are still only tentative. The Turks had no systematic organization above battalion level, and it has been said that the Sultan was forced to turn to the British ambassador to get an up-to-date order of battle at the outbreak of war.

As for the Turkish war plan, if there was one it never became apparent. The senior army commanders conducted their operations with blithe disregard for each other. Indeed, the Ottoman high command was driven by factional rivalry, and many officers spent more time intriguing against their fellow generals than fighting the Russians.

Nevertheless, whatever the precise number of Turkish soldiers serving in the region in the summer of 1877, there were more of them, and they fought harder, than the Russians had bargained for.

Crossing the Danube

The Russian plan began promisingly with a well-managed deployment through Romania. General M.I. Dragomirov crossed the Danube successfully in an operation notable for its thorough staffwork and preparatory reconnaissance – features which were to become increasingly rare as the campaign continued. By 1 July four Russian corps were south of the Danube, heading for their objectives. IX Corps was marching on Nikopolis; XII and XIII Corps were heading for the line of the River Jantra, from which they would advance on Rushchuk; and VIII Corps was driving directly for Tirnovo. XI and IV Corps formed a general reserve on the north bank of the Danube opposite Sistova.

Ahead of the infantry formations raced a flying column under Major General V. I. Gourko, the former commander of 2nd Guards Division. Grand Duke Nicholas had despatched Gourko with some 16,000 men to seize the passes through the Balkan mountains before the Turks could organize their defences. Gourko's force was based around ten battalions of light infantry: the 4th Rifle Brigade and the Bulgarian Legion, plus a half-battalion of dismounted Cossacks. His detachment also included two regiments of dragoons and four of Cossacks, together with two horse artillery and two mountain batteries. After two days of fighting, Gourko captured the Shipka Pass on 7 July; and there he remained for two weeks, while Turkish reinforcements assembled south of the mountains. There was no sign of the main Russian army.

Tsar Alexander II had decided to join his army in the field. This brought about a strange paralysis in the Russian high command; the boldness that had characterized the initial invasion was replaced by caution of the worst kind. Furthermore, the vast Imperial entourage demanded 17 trains or up to 500 wagons to move itself – a most unwelcome burden for the army's logistic organization.

The initial crossing of the Danube, and Gourko's raid, were later to be celebrated by Soviet military historians as model combined-arms operations. The two lines of Turkish natural defences, the Danube and the Balkan mountains, had been penetrated in a matter of weeks. However, the Tsar and his military advisors regarded a headlong advance on the Ottoman capital as too great a risk while substantial Ottoman forces remained in northern Bulgaria. VIII Corps was halted at Tirnovo awaiting IV and XI Corps.

Nikopolis was stormed by Krüdener's IX Corps on 16 July, while XII and XIII Corps found themselves confronted by an unexpectedly active Turkish defence, conducted by Mehemet Ali, along the line of the River Lom. Krüdener learned that a Turkish force had occupied Plevna, 25 miles away and perilously close to the Russian line of communication to the Balkan passes. He despatched his 5th Infantry Division under Lt. Gen. Shilder-Schuldner, which assaulted the Turkish position at 4.00 am on 20 July.

The Russian assault on Plevna collapsed in the face of heavy fire from entrenched Turkish infantry. Osman Pasha had force-marched 11,000 men from Vidin – travelling 110 miles over bad roads in only 6½ days – and now outnumbered the attackers by almost two to one. The Russians lost 3,000 men including one brigade and two regimental commanders. A week's forced march followed by digging-in left Osman's soldiers utterly exhausted, however, so an aggressive pursuit was out of the question. Krüdener's entire corps was now ordered to Plevna to try again.

The Second Battle of Plevna

While the Russians assembled their forces before Plevna Osman Pasha's soldiers strengthened their positions, constructing a series of large redoubts connected by entrenchments. Stragglers from Osman's forced march arrived in Plevna, and a further eight battalions arrived from Sophia. Leaving six battalions and a battery to keep open his line of communications, Osman Pasha had available 33 battalions, 5 squadrons and 58 guns – a total of 22,000 men – when Krüdener attacked again on 30 July. For the second battle of Plevna the Russians had some 35,000 men: 36 battalions, 30 squadrons and 170 guns. This included the whole of IX Corps, less the 18th Infantry Regiment, which had suffered catastrophic losses in the first assault. IV and XI Corps each provided an extra brigade, and Krüdener was also supported by the flamboyant Gen. Mikhail Skoboleff and his Cossack brigade.

A Russian infantryman in the campaign dress worn by the Guards, Grenadiers, Rifles and some line divisions. Note the gaiters, and the pioneer sword he has acquired in addition to his (permanently fixed) bayonet. (Author's Collection)

Baron Krüdener was the only Russian corps commander with no previous experience of active service. Two weeks before he had stormed Nikopolis against light opposition, and seems to have hoped to succeed again in a similar manner on 30 July; without reconnaissance, he plunged his command into a headlong assault on the Turkish lines. The Russian artillery conducted a long-range bombardment, but against the enemy's deep, narrow trenches this was completely ineffective. Equally, it failed to inflict much damage on the main Turkish strongpoints. The Russian infantry battalions attacked in close order with possibly only ten per cent of the men actually using their rifles: the rest charged forward with fixed bayonets. The thin skirmish screen had no chance of establishing fire superiority over the defenders, and the shoulder-to-shoulder formations behind were cut to pieces by Turkish fire. Russian casualties amounted to over 7,000, with some regiments losing over half their effective strength. Although some of the Turkish trenches south of Plevna were overrun at one point, Turkish counter-attacks restored the line before nightfall. The second battle of Plevna cost the Russians 23 per cent of their soldiers and 25 per cent of their officers. Turkish losses were approximately 2,000, but were made good within a few days by the arrival of four more battalions and a draft of replacements.

The disaster at Plevna completely derailed the Russian plan of operations. The six corps (IV, VIII, IX, XI, XII and XIII) south of the Danube faced substantial Turkish forces in the west at Plevna and in the east around Razgrad. A third Turkish army was now reported to the south. There was no possibility of continuing the offensive, but it would have been politically ruinous to abandon the Bulgarians to the vengeance of the Turks. The Russian high command was left with no option but to hold on to their gains and summon reinforcements from Russia. Four days after the catastrophe at Plevna, Alexander II ordered the mobilization of the Imperial Guard Corps, the two Grenadier divisions and two more line divisions. The first *ban* of the militia was also

The epic defensive battles at Plevna halted the Russian offensive in its tracks. Russian prestige was severely damaged, and the chances of Great Power intervention began

called out to replace battle casualties, and three divisions of the reserve were placed on active duty to occupy garrisons vacated by the troops now heading for the front.

Slaughter in the Shipka Pass

While the Russians battered away at Plevna the Turks were assembling a large army south of the Balkans. Suleiman Pasha's army had arrived by sea and was reinforced with local troops to give him between 30,000 and 40,000 men. He could have crossed the mountains by one of the eastern passes and combined with Mehemet Ali's forces, which were driving the Russian left wing back towards the River Jantra; but Suleiman despised Mehemet Ali – a German soldier-of-fortune born Jules Détroit – and was determined to recapture the Shipka Pass. The Russians' seizure of this key strategic position had caused great alarm in Constantinople, and the commander who retook it would undoubtedly be handsomely rewarded by the Sultan.

Rising to an altitude of 5,000 feet above sea level, the Shipka Pass follows a tortuous path along a ridge line for about ten miles. Dominated by the surrounding mountains, it is the best route from northern Bulgaria to the city of Adrianople and Constantinople itself. In August 1877 it was held by 4,400 troops: three battalions of the Orel Regiment, five battalions of the Bulgarian Legion, a detachment of engineers, and 27 guns. The nearest supports were the VIII Corps, whose leading elements were nearly 30 miles away towards Tirnovo.

On 21 August Suleiman unleashed his army in a frontal assault as unco-ordinated and as unsuccessful as the first Russian attacks on Plevna. For the next five days, wave after wave of Turkish infantry charged the Russian entrenchments and were mown down. On the spur of Mount St. Nicholas the Russians had established a redoubt with a battery of Krupp guns captured from the Turks: this drew the heaviest assaults of all. The defenders' ammunition ran out at one point, and they were reduced to rolling

to increase. Here Russian soldiers are shown surging into a Turkish redoubt; in reality most were usually shot down hundreds of yards away. (Author's Collection)

The defence of the 'Eagle's Eyrie' at Shipka Pass; the Russian defenders, running low on ammunition, resorted to throwing rocks at the Turks. The defenders were saved by reinforcements arriving just in time, including infantrymen who hitched rides on the backs of the cavalry's horses. (Author's Collection)

boulders down on to the Turks scrambling up the hillside. The Turkish soldiers fought with fanatical bravery, but their senior officers displayed no tactical skill and persisted in hurling their men at the strongest part of the enemy line. As for the Russians, never has the legendary stubbornness of the Russian soldier been more clearly demonstrated. In an apparently hopeless position, almost surrounded by an enemy infamous for their treatment of wounded and prisoners, the Russians were prepared to fight to the last man. The Bulgarian Legion fought with equal determination, no doubt aware of the fate that awaited them if they surrendered. On 23 August the 4th Rifle Brigade arrived from Tirnovo in the nick of time, the leading battalion having 'hitched a ride' on Cossack ponies. By 25 August five more infantry regiments had arrived, and Suleiman Pasha withdrew to Kazanlik shortly afterwards. He had expended the lives of about 10,000 Turkish soldiers at the Shipka Pass; Russian losses totalled 3,640.

The Third Battle of Plevna

During Suleiman's desperate attacks at Shipka the Russians began to prepare for a great assault on the Turkish army at Plevna. The two previous defeats had seriously damaged Russian prestige and it was thought politically expedient to capture the town quickly, without waiting for the Guards and Grena-

diers on their way from Russia. Twelve 24-pdr. siege guns were ordered from Sistova, as the 9-pdr. field guns had proved ineffective against the Turkish earthworks. As a curtain-raiser for the main offensive Maj. Gen. Prince Imeretinski attacked the small town of Lovtcha, ten miles from Plevna. Defended by about 8,000 Turks, Lovtcha controlled an important road junction, and its capture would isolate Plevna altogether.

Imeretinski commanded a mixed force of 25 battalions, 14 squadrons and 98 guns – a total of 27,000 men. Although his subordinate Skoboleff estimated the Turkish strength at nearer 15,000 (and went on to claim all credit for the subsequent victory himself), it was Imeretinski who captured the Turkish position. Over 2,000 Turks were killed on the field and another 4,000 were cut down by the Cossack brigade as they fled towards Plevna. Russian losses were 319 dead and 1,197 wounded. After the war the action at Lovtcha came to be regarded as a textbook example of how to attack entrenched infantry armed with modern weapons. The operation was notable for its prior reconnaissance and thorough artillery preparation, with 4,883 shells fired in support of the attack. The infantry attacked in more open formations, reserves were fed in to exploit success, and the enemy was pursued with vigour. However, if the action at Lovtcha showed that the Russians were

Grand Duke Nicholas Nicholaevich was renowned for his colourful personal life – using the field telegraph in Bulgaria to communicate with an opera singer in St. Petersburg was typical. But he presided over two bold strokes: the initial invasion, and the winter march over the Balkan mountains. (Author's Collection)

in their trenches, and met each assault with a hail of fire from Martini-Peabody breechloaders and Winchester repeating rifles. In the northern sector the Romanian and Russian troops succeeded in gaining a temporary lodgement in the Grivitsa redoubts, but their losses were severe, and by nightfall the attackers were extremely disorganized. The central section of the Turkish line held all day, inflicting heavy losses on the 16th and 39th Infantry Divisions, which persisted in attacking in company columns.

The only Russian success of the day came in the south, where Gen. Skoboleff led Imeretinski's first echelon. Mounted on a white charger and wearing a white coat, Skoboleff attracted the attention of many Turkish riflemen, and most of his staff were hit. (His horse was killed too – the fifth time he had been shot off his horse in battle.) With 13 guns in close support of his infantry, Skoboleff overran the redoubts protecting the southern outskirts of Plevna. Unfortunately his men were left on their own, disorganized by their own success and having suffered serious losses. Calls for reinforcements went unheeded; and although Skoboleff brought forward two guns and collected about a thousand stragglers during the night, the Turks were allowed to counter-attack in the morning without interference from the rest of the Russian army. By midday on 12 September the Russian army was back in its old positions, having suffered 12,800 casualties including 300 officers; the Romanian army lost another 3,000. Turkish casualties were estimated at 4,000, mostly in the southern sector.

The third defeat at Plevna sapped Russian morale, and had grave political as well as military consequences. Russian stock collapsed on the continental exchanges, and Russian paper money was discounted by over a third of its face value. Banks throughout Europe refused to float Russian war loans.

Plevna Besieged

With a further assault out of the question, the Russian high command decided to surround Plevna and starve its defenders into submission. The reinforcements would arrive shortly, and Gen. Todleben of Sevastopol fame was appointed to organize the formal siege of Plevna. Prince Imeretinski and Gen. Skoboleff were both promoted: the former became

learning, they confounded foreign observers within weeks by another disastrous assault on Plevna itself.

Bolstered by the arrival of Prince Charles of Romania at the head of 32,000 Romanian troops, the Russians had some 84,000 soldiers and 424 guns in place for their set-piece attack. Scheduled for the Tsar's name-day on 11 September, it was preceded by a four-day artillery barrage, with harassing fire maintained throughout the night to frustrate Turkish attempts to repair the damage to their defences. Thick ground fog obscured most of the battlefield on the day scheduled for the grand assault. It turned to a steady drizzle as the Russian and Romanian infantry rose from their positions to charge the Turkish lines.

Once again there was little co-ordination between the infantry and artillery, and the Turks inflicted heavy losses on the attackers. They had stockpiled large reserves of small arms ammunition chief-of-staff of the western army whilst his head-strong subordinate received the command of 16th Infantry Division. Conversely, the commanders of XI and XIII Corps, Gens. Shakofskoi and Hahn, were both dismissed, being replaced by Prince Korsakoff and Baron Dellingshausen. There were numerous promotions throughout the army, and Tsar Alexander showered all ranks with decorations – although the number awarded to the already be-medalled hangers-on at his headquarters drew un-favourable comments from the frontline soldiers.

For his part, Osman Pasha could see the writing on the wall. His army was too outnumbered to prevent the Russians overwhelming him in Plevna, and he applied to the Sultan for permission to withdraw. However, the Ottoman Defence Council seemed to have decided that Plevna had to be held at all costs. Like Verdun or Stalingrad in the World Wars, it had assumed a political importance out of all proportion to its strategic value. If the rest of the Turkish armies had taken a more active role in operations such a strategy might have proved suc-cessful. Probably suspecting what would actually happen, however, Osman re-deployed his troops to try to keep open the road to Sophia. He reinforced his garrisons at Dolni Dubnik, Gorni Dubnik and Telish.

Meanwhile, Suleiman Pasha renewed his at-tempts to break through the Shipka Pass. He brought up siege mortars to lob shells vertically into the Russian battery on Mount St. Nicholas, bombarding the strongpoint from 13 to 16 September. In the early hours of 17 September a picked force of 3,500 Turkish infantry climbed up the hillsides and launched a surprise attack. They captured the sum-mit, and by dawn the red crescent banner was flying over the Shipka Pass. Suleiman telegraphed Con-stantinople with news of his triumph – but unfortu-nately for him, and the volunteer assault troops, his subordinate commanders failed miserably. Support-ing attacks either failed or never took place. A large

part of the army remained in camp all day. Gen. Radetsky organized a series of bruising counter-attacks, and after desperate bayonet fighting on the mountain-top the Turks on Mount St. Nicholas were driven back and their bodies hurled over the edge. The Russians estimated Turkish losses at over 3,000; the south side of the mountain was strewn with corpses.

Suleiman reverted to sniping and occasional mortar barrages; but on 2 October his intrigues against Mehemet Ali finally bore fruit. He was appointed to replace Mehemet as commander of the Army of the Quadrilateral. Reouf Pasha, Minister of Marine, succeeded Suleiman in command of the luckless Turkish soldiers at Shipka.

Gen. Gourko, whose capture of the pass had led to this bitter battle in the mountains, had been ordered back to St. Petersburg to supervise the mobilisation of the Guard cavalry. He returned to Bulgaria in time to lead a series of attacks on Osman Pasha's communications. On 20 October the Impe-rial Guard arrived at Plevna. Gourko was given command of 35,000 infantry, 10,000 cavalry and 48 guns, including the 1st and 2nd Guard Infantry Divisions and the Guard Rifle Brigade, the 2nd Guard Cavalry Division and an engineer battalion.

On 24 October Gourko attacked Gorni Dubnik. The 3,500 Turkish defenders put up a terrific fight

Russian studies of the American Civil War concluded that long-distance cavalry raids could play an important strategic role. Gourko, commander of the Guard Cavalry, led just such a raid in 1877, seizing the Shipka Pass. He was less successful at Plevna, launching costly frontal attacks on outlying Turkish positions. (Author's Collection)

against overwhelming odds, holding out until nightfall; about 1,500 Turks were killed before the survivors surrendered. Six Turkish battalions and just four guns had inflicted 3,211 casualties on the Guard; the Guard Grenadiers and the Paul Regiment each lost a third of their strength.

Meanwhile the Life Guard Jäger Regiment (four battalions), supported by two cavalry brigades and 20 guns, assaulted the nearby strongpoint at Telish, where seven battalions of Turks were dug in. The Guardsmen came under fire at over 1,000 yards from the position; they pressed home their attack with tremendous courage, getting to within 100 yards of the main trenches before being driven to ground. By that afternoon they were beaten back with the loss of 26 officers and 907 other ranks.

Losing so many of the Tsar's beloved guardsmen to no good purpose nearly cost Gourko his career. After uncomfortable interviews with both the Emperor and the Grand Duke, Gourko surrounded the Turkish posts at Telish and Dolni Dubnik, conducted a thorough reconnaissance, and brought up more artillery. The defenders of Telish surrendered after 72 guns fired some 3,000 rounds into their positions on 28 October; the bombardment inflicted 157 casualties, and the Russians captured about 3,000 prisoners, four guns and a vast quantity of small arms ammunition intended for Osman Pasha. When they heard of the surrender, the five battalions at Dolni Dubnik withdrew into Plevna.

By mid-November Osman Pasha's army was besieged by over 120,000 Russians and Romanians with 522 guns. The town was under constant bombardment, resulting in numerous civilian casualties; in their dug-outs the Turkish soldiers were harder to hit than the unfortunate inhabitants. Food was running out and conditions in the field hospitals were indescribable. On 10 December the desperate Turks made a determined attempt to break out, and after ferocious assaults overran the Russian frontline trenches. There was a second line of entrenchments behind, however, and the Russian artillery exacted a heavy toll. Osman Pasha himself was wounded, and the Russian and Romanian forces counter-attacked, breaking into the Turkish defences. The Turks surrendered Plevna that afternoon.

This desperate last throw cost the Turks approximately 6,000 casualties, against Russian and Romanian losses of around 1,200. Just over 43,000 Turkish soldiers passed into captivity, and the Russians also captured 77 field guns and immense quantities of small arms ammunition. The Turkish prisoners were subjected to the same sort of death-march as Marshal Paulus' men at Stalingrad in 1943: herded back to Russia in the depth of winter, deprived of food, water and adequate clothing, few of them returned to Turkey after the war. The defenders of Plevna were paying the price for earlier Turkish atrocities: wounded Russian prisoners had been killed on several battlefields, and the dead mutilated.

The seizure of the vital Shipka Pass was a severe blow to the Turks. In an attempt to recapture it, a large Turkish army was assembled south of the Balkans under Suleiman Pasha. He presided over a succession of uncoordinated frontal attacks that cost thousands of lives. (Author's Collection)

Neither side welcomed captives in this bitter war; Gen. Skoboleff made it plain to his new division that prisoners were not to be taken.

The Winter Campaign

Bulgaria was already in the grip of winter by the time Plevna fell. Within days of the capitulation the Danube began to freeze, breaking the Russian pontoon bridge and temporarily isolating the entire army. But there was no thought of going into winter quarters. Once again, political considerations were paramount: further delay was bound to lead to great power intervention, and the Russian command decided on a winter campaign through the Balkan mountains and on to Constantinople.

In eastern Bulgaria the large Turkish forces based on the fortresses of the Quadrilateral had remained inactive after a brief offensive in September. Facing the Russian XI, XII and XIII Corps Mehemet Ali had over 50,000 troops at his disposal, but was constantly undermined by his fellow officers. (His forces included the Egyptian contingent under Prince Hassan – a favourite of the Sultan whose division had retreated from the battlefield of Cerkovna on 21 September after just four men were killed and 30 wounded!) Suleiman Pasha succeeded Mehemet Ali in October, but did not take the offensive until late November when Plevna's fate was already sealed. Even then, his drive petered out within days after a few minor clashes. The Russian left flank was secure.

At the southern end of the Shipka Pass there were some 35,000 Turkish troops and 108 guns commanded by Vessil Pasha. The Russians re-organized their vast host around Plevna into three columns. Gen. Gourko, with 65,000 troops, was ordered to break through the Araba Konak Pass and occupy Sophia. Gen. Radetzky confronted the Turks at Shipka with 56,000 men, while the remaining Russian forces masked the Ottoman army in eastern Bulgaria and laid siege to Rustchuk.

As the temperature fell to 3°F by night, Gourko's men embarked on an epic march through the mountain snows. Outflanking the fortified Turkish positions, his men reached Sophia on 4 January, driving out a small garrison and the Turkish civilian population. Despite the most appalling weather conditions Gourko had broken the Turkish defences,

According to one of the more salacious diaries of the war, Suleiman Pasha began his military career by occupying 'a very doubtful position in the household of an old Pasha'. In 1877 he spent more time scheming against fellow Ottoman generals than fighting the Russians. Blamed for the débâcle in 1878, he was sentenced to 15 years in a military fortress. (Author's Collection)

and a rapid march on Philipopolis threatened to cut off the Turkish troops holding the Trojan Pass.

Radetzky opened his own offensive on 5 January despite ten-foot-deep snow drifts along the mountain paths. He divided his forces into three columns, gambling correctly that the Turks were relying on the weather to defend them. Travelling on parallel routes through the mountains, the left column was commanded by Prince Mirksy, the centre by Radetsky and the right by Skoboleff. The centre made little progress against the main Turkish defences. Mirsky's men captured the village of Shipka in the face of heavy opposition. Menaced by Turkish reserves, Mirsky was left waiting for Skoboleff, whose troops arrived at the proverbial last moment to encircle the Turkish forces. On 9 January Skoboleff's men stormed the redoubts at Sheinovo in the sort of headlong assault that had so often failed earlier in the war. It was a dramatic stroke that boosted his reputation to new levels, although there is some evidence that he deliberately delayed his arrival so that his division could save the day. Vessil Pasha's

Left: Turkish infantry went to war in a Zouave-style uniform of fez, jacket and baggy trousers. Line infantry battalions had red trim, light infantry had green. Gaiters and shoes were the most common footwear, but some soldiers had long boots. (Author's Collection)

Right: A lieutenant-general by the age of 33, Skoboleff was a veteran of Russia's colonial wars in Central Asia – to which he would return until his death in 1882. Although lionized by the British correspondents and his own soldiers, his rabid Pan-Slavism and thirst for personal glory alienated many fellow officers. (Author's Collection)

army laid down its arms, and another 33,000 Turks passed into wretched captivity.

Turkish forces south of the Balkans were once again under the command of the arch-intriguer Suleiman Pasha. Ordered back from the army in eastern Bulgaria and the supine garrisons of the Quadrilateral fortresses, Suleiman found himself outnumbered two to one by Gourko's army advancing from Sophia. Part of the Turkish army under Fuad Pasha conducted a model rearguard action on the road to Philipopolis, during which the British commander Valentine Baker Pasha distinguished himself; but in the ensuing clash between the main armies from 15 to 17 January Suleiman's troops were routed. Adrianople fell without a struggle, and the Russian army was free to march on Constantinople. Turkey sued for peace as a Royal Navy squadron passed through the Dardanelles to guarantee the security of the Turkish capital. Although the Russians were encamped outside Constantinople by February, their fears of great power intervention had at last been realized.

The Treaty of San Stefano, signed between Russia and Turkey on 3 March 1878, was to be re-written later in Berlin. No European power was prepared to accept the terms Russia imposed on Turkey, and the full fruits of the Russian military victory were lost at the negotiating table.

War in the Caucasus

The full story of the Caucasian theatre of operations is too long to recount in detail. Suffice to say that here too the initial Russian offensive was boldly conducted before the full strength of the Turkish position became apparent. Grand Duke Mikhail had about 50,000 men facing up to twice that number of Turks. He was reinforced in July with the 1st Grenadier Division and the 40th Infantry Division, and launched an offensive against the main Turkish army in September.

General Obruchoff, the officer responsible for Russia's pre-war planning, was posted to the Caucasian theatre in time to lead the Russian attack. Although an initial three-day battle was inconclusive, the Turkish commander, Muktiar Pasha, withdrew. The Russians then divided their forces, and by keeping their lines of communication in touch by telegraph, were able to attack the Turks in their new positions from the front and flank simultaneously, in a classic pincer movement. The Turks were heavily defeated, suffering 16,000 casualties and losing 8,500 prisoners. In November, Grand Duke Mikhail conducted a well-planned night assault on the fortress of Kars; diversionary efforts drew off the Turkish reserves after several nights of feint attacks and bombardments, and at a cost of 2,270 men, the Russians

Above: Gen. Mikhail Skoboleff leads his men into the Turkish defences, mounted on his white charger. Skoboleff was the only Russian commander to make any progress during the great October assault on Plevna. His *bravery – and assiduous courting of British journalists – made him the most highly regarded of the Tsar's generals. (Author's Collection)*

captured the Turks' most modern fortress. Erzerzoum was besieged shortly afterwards, and was surrendered in March under the provisions of the San Stefano treaty; but cholera and typhoid had already broken out in the siege lines, and both armies suffered badly.

THE RUSSIAN ARMY

The political crisis of 1876 caught the Russian army in a period of transition. Only two years earlier its traditional system of recruiting – with conscripts chosen to serve almost the whole of their working lives – had been changed to a more modern scheme inspired by the German army. This reorganization was part of a series of profound reforms undertaken by Tsar Alexander II. In 1861 he had emancipated the Empire's 23 million serfs, hitherto tied to the

land (and the landowners) by law, and still bound to the Tsar by centuries of mystical religious tradition. The social, legal and political changes engineered by Alexander II were designed to transform Russia and to enable the Empire to keep pace with the great powers of Europe. However, while Russia's institutions were to be modernized, the Tsar remained determined to retain the regime's monopoly of political power.

The sheer size of the Russian army has been a key factor in central and south-west European political and military calculations ever since the 18th century; yet in the 1870s Russia's antiquated military structure left it effectively outnumbered by its potential adversaries. Russian planners were acutely conscious that both Germany and Austria-Hungary could mobilize larger armies – and could deploy them to the frontiers far faster than the lumbering Russian war machine. In both cases better administration and a far more extensive railway network gave Russia's most likely enemies a substantial advantage. Russia's problem was that although it had a large standing army, it was difficult to expand it in wartime due to the lack of a modern reserve system. By contrast, the Prussian army could treble its size on mobilization; even the French army doubled when it recalled short-service conscripts to active duty.

From 1875 Russian conscripts were to serve six years with the colours and nine in reserve, although in practice they would actually be furloughed for the fifth and sixth years of active duty. Hitherto peasants selected for conscription had served for 25 years – and the landowners naturally ensured that the army received those peasants they could best spare. On mobilization, men who had left the colours within two years returned to bring units of the active army up to their wartime strength. Those who had left between two and six years beforehand would be used to replace battle casualties. Those who had passed into the reserve six to nine years previously would form separate reserve battalions that could, for example, relieve active battalions from garrison duty.

Above: The Tsarevitch presided over a lacklustre Russian performance in eastern Bulgaria. His forces masked the Turkish fortresses of the Quadrilateral. (Author's Collection)

Left: A Russian officer directs the firing line with customary disregard for his own safety. By the autumn of 1877 the Russians were forced to draft cavalry officers into many infantry regiments because of catastrophic officer casualties. (Author's Collection)

Russian military administration improved enormously after the Crimean War, and in 1877 the Russian army finally succeeded in reaching Constantinople without being decimated by disease. Deaths from disease reached 37 men per thousand in 1855, but fell to 17.6 by 1871, and would drop to 10.4 by 1879. Army morale improved, with recorded disciplinary offences dropping from 17,000 in 1871 to 9,000 in 1876. Savage corporal punishments were still available under the Russian disciplinary code, but officers had little occasion to resort to them.

Infantry organization

In 1877 the Russian army consisted of 47 active infantry divisions: three Guard, four Grenadier, 40 line and one Caucasian. Each division consisted of four infantry regiments, each of three battalions. It had been decided to expand regiments to four battalions as early as 1873, but the reorganization had hardly started when war was declared. Another 1873 decision – to add two brigade HQs to each division –

had also barely begun to be implemented. Most divisions had no such subordinate headquarters units during the war.

Each battalion comprised four line companies and one 'sharpshooter' (*strelkovaia*) company. A full-strength company was made up as follows: one captain, one lieutenant, one sub-lieutenant, one ensign, one 'junker' (candidate for commission), four senior sergeants, 12 junior non-commissioned officers, 20 lance corporals, 148 privates, one pay-sergeant, three drummers, three buglers, one armourer-sergeant, 12 privates-in-reserve, one apothecary, one apprentice apothecary, and four officers' servants – total strength: 215 officers and men. A regiment's regulation war strength was 76 officers, 270 non-commissioned officers, 70 musicians, 2,700 combatant rank and file, five clerks, 154 non-combatant rank and file, plus 41 wagons and 174 horses.

Armament

The war also caught the Russian infantry in the middle of re-arming: four different rifles were in service, and the two in most widespread use had incompatible ammunition. It is a typically Russian irony that this unsatisfactory state of affairs stemmed not from technological backwardness, but from the army's eagerness to modernize. Senior officers were determined to avoid a repetition of the Crimean catastrophe: at the Alma and Inkerman Russian soldiers with muskets had been shot down by rifle-armed enemies at ranges of several hundred yards, far beyond the reach of the Russians' smoothbores.

In 1857 the Russian army adopted the *Vintovka* .60 calibre rifled muzzle-loader; over 250,000 were bought from German and Belgian factories. But the startling success of the Prussian Dreyse needle-gun in 1866 alerted the Russian command to the power of breechloading weapons. Acting with commendable speed, within twelve months the War Ministry bought 200,000 Karle rifles – rifled muzzle-loaders converted to breechloading by a Swedish inventor. Unfortunately, the Karle was one of the less successful of the many conversion systems then competing for business; so Grand Duke Nicholai Alexandrovich privately funded the purchase of 10,000 Baranov rifles – a Russian trapdoor breechloading conversion which seemed far more reliable. However, after conducting a series of service trials, the War Ministry

Mehemet Ali Pasha, commander of Turkish forces in eastern Bulgaria until unseated by Suleiman's intrigues. Born Jules Détroit, he was a German of Huguenot descent who came from Magdeburg. He won promotion after defeating Serbian rebels before the war, and was assassinated in 1879 during counter-insurgency operations in Albania. (Author's Collection)

selected one of the many breechloading conversions developed by the Czech inventor Slyvester Krnk. The Krnk's highly competitive price played no small part in its selection, so the Russian soldier – like so many before and since – would have cause to remember that he was armed with the weapon made by the lowest bidder.

The Krnk was ordered in 1869, by which date yet another weapon was already under examination. Two Russian officers spent 1867–9 in America studying US designs, especially those of Hiram Berdan, the gun designer and commander of the Federal sharpshooter regiment in the Civil War. The War Ministry bought several thousand of a .42 calibre breechloader which it designated the 'Model 1868' but which is also known as the 'Berdan 1'. In 1869 Berdan visited St. Petersburg with a new design, a single-shot bolt-action .40 calibre rifle which was demonstrably superior to any weapon in Russian service. This 'Berdan II' fired the first military cartridge with an outside centre-fire Berdan primer

The bolt-action Berdan II was issued to the Guards, Grenadiers, Rifles and some line infantry divisions in 1877. Far superior to the Krnk, it had only begun to enter service in quantity since 1875. (Author's Collection)

and a bottlenecked case. It fired a 370 grain bullet at 1,450 feet per second, and its flat trajectory impressed observers from both Britain and France. Despite its commitment to the Krnk, the War Ministry ordered the Berdan II in 1871. It took three years to assemble the necessary machine tooling at Tula and Izhevsk for domestic manufacture, and an interim order was placed with the Birmingham Small Arms Company for 30,000 rifles. By 1877 the Guards, Grenadiers, Rifle battalions and some line regiments were armed with the *Berdanka*, as it was christened; most line troops still had the Krnk, however.

Uniforms

With its organization and armament in a state of flux, it is perhaps not surprising that even the uniforms of the Russian army were undergoing radical change during the 1870s. Nicholas I had approved a new French-style uniform in 1855, the old coatee being replaced by a tunic and a shako substituted for the line infantry's spiked helmet. Alexander II continued the process, introducing a cloth kepi for other ranks in 1864. From 1872 officers were supposed to wear an Austrian-style stiff kepi with gold braid on the top. However, many regiments retained the *furashka* or

forage cap, and the kepi was never fully adopted. Resistance was led by the Guards regiments and by the Pan-Slavists in the army, who opposed foreign-inspired uniforms on principle. It says much for the strength of Pan-Slav feeling that it could find expression in the army's uniform – and that officers were prepared to defy the Tsar over the issue.

From 1872 soldiers wore a single-breasted green tunic, with green trousers in winter and white ones in summer. However, campaigning in Central Asia led to the adoption of a white canvas blouse, 'the perfection of a campaign garment', according to a British observer; 'the white was not so pronounced as to dazzle in the sunshine, nor did the dust of the road and stain of the bivouac foul it to absolute dinginess. It could be washed and dried in an hour and it was loose enough to allow thick underclothing to be worn under it when the burning heat turned suddenly to searching chilliness.' White linen cap covers were introduced at the same time, presenting a dramatic alternative to the 'official' uniform.

The official service dress included shoulder boards (*pogoni*) which, from 1871, displayed the regimental number; the number of the battalion was indicated on the kepi. This proved very useful to the more enterprising Turkish officers, as Baker Pasha observed: 'From the numbers on the shoulder knots and the kepis of the dead we could tell precisely the regiments and brigades which had been engaged . . . [which] gave rise to reflection whether this marking of regiments when on active service was not a mistake. The Turkish dead gave no clue as to which force they belonged to.'

In 1877 Russian infantrymen still wrapped their feet in linen cloths instead of socks – a practice that would survive for another hundred years. Long boots were worn throughout the army, traditionally loose-fitting so that they could be packed with insulating straw during winter. Greatcoats, worn in blanket roll style during warm weather, were supplied with a hood (*bashlik*) for winter wear; this was very similar to that worn by Turkish troops, and the infantrymen of both sides looked very similar in full winter kit. However, while the Turkish generals relied on the winter snows to keep the Russians at bay, the Russian army fought its way over the Balkans despite atrocious conditions. Some Russian regiments suffered severely in the process; the Podolian Regiment, for example, lost 900 men to frostbite in three weeks. Russian winter uniforms were robust and as warm as 19th century technology allowed, but they were of limited value in prolonged winter warfare. Fighting commanders like Gen. Radetzky shared the hardships of their troops, earning their respect and inspiring them to incredible feats of endurance.

The infantrymen's leather equipment was all black. Two cartridge boxes, each holding 15 rounds, were worn on the front of the belt; another 60 rounds were carried in the large haversack. Officers and colour-sergeants were issued with a Smith & Wesson .44 'Russian' single-action revolver carried in a black leather flap-over holster and secured by a lanyard. The Russian army contract was a considerable coup for Smith & Wesson, who delivered over 140,000

weapons during the 1870s.

A Russian infantryman's uniform was made up and fitted at company level. This practice of local assembly made possible the wide variations on official style, and the political outlook of the officers determined how 'Slavic' a regiment appeared. The general appearance of the Russian army in 1877 contrasted sharply with that in the Napoleonic or Crimean wars, and anticipated the Russian military uniforms of the 20th century.

Cavalry organisation

In 1877 the Russian army included 19 cavalry divisions: two Guards, two Cossack, one Caucasian and 14 line. The latter consisted of one regiment each of dragoons, uhlans and hussars. A cavalry regiment consisted of 33 officers, 64 non-commissioned offi-

Russian officers were issued with the Smith & Wesson 'Russian' .44 single-action revolver. A latch on the top-strap breaks the action, allowing the barrel to swing down and the ejector star to lift the empty cases clear of the cylinder. (Author's Collection)

cers, 17 trumpeters, 512 mounted men and 120 dismounted men, five clerks, 135 non-combatants, 13 wagons, 55 draught horses and 593 horses. Cossack regiments had a different structure: 21 officers, 86 non-commissioned officers, 19 trumpeters, 685 men, one clerk, 41 non-combatants, 75 draught horses and 802 troop horses. Regiments were divided into four squadrons, which were the preferred tactical unit. Cossack regiments were divided into six *sotnias*.

Armament

In 1869 the Russian army introduced new drill regulations for its cavalry, the first since 1845. However, these seemed to take no account of the Crimean War or more recent conflicts in Europe or America; they emphasized shock action, and disregarded the possibility of fighting dismounted. Within a few years this traditional view of cavalry operations was challenged within the War Ministry by studies of the American Civil War. Some officers concluded that long-distance raids were the true function of cavalry now that battlefields were dominated by breechloading rifles. From 1871 the dra-

goon regiments were re-armed with rifles and began to train as mounted infantry, in contrast to the practice of most European powers. Dismounted drill for hussar and uhlan regiments was introduced two years later.

Issued with Berdan or Krnk rifles and charges of gun cotton for demolition purposes, Russian line cavalry divisions were trained to act far in advance of the main body of the army, penetrating deep behind enemy lines in the manner of Grierson or Bedford Forrest. On exercises before the war in Vilnius district a division rode 170km in two days before going into action. While some exercises revealed that a high proportion of the conscript horsemen were unaccustomed to long spells in the saddle, the Russian cavalry was unusually well prepared for war in 1877.

The front ranks of hussar and uhlan regiments were armed with lances, swords and revolvers, the second ranks with rifles; all men in the dragoon regiments carried rifles. For dismounted action one man in three acted as a horse-holder. Prolonged firefights were clearly not anticipated, as rifle-armed cavalrymen carried only 20 rounds each.

A Russian officer goes down fighting in a contemporary print which shows the uniforms of both sides with reasonable accuracy. Russian officers were easily distinguished from their men by their cleaner, brighter white jackets. (Author's Collection)

Uniforms

While the infantry fought the war in modern-looking uniforms, it is no surprise to record that the senior Russian cavalry regiments took the field in their traditional splendour. A Prussian officer serving in a Russian infantry regiment saw 'officers of the guard with their uniforms looking as new and as smart as when in the Nevski Prospekt at St. Petersburg, especially the Guard Hussars in their gold-braided red tunics, scarcely distinguishable from the Prussian Guard Hussars . . . champagne flowed in streams at their table.' If their uniforms harked back to a glorious history, so did their tactical value; apart from chasing away any Turkish irregular horse that became too inquisitive, the Guard cavalry made little impact on the battlefields of Bulgaria.

Hussars

The Russo-Turkish was the last conflict in which the hussar regiments were to take part before they disappeared for a generation. In 1882 all but the two Guards regiments were converted to dragoons;

Nicholas II would later revive the old regimental identities in the wake of the Russo-Japanese war. By 1877 pelisses had been replaced by an Attila, and all regiments wore a kepi with drooping black plume. Regimental distinctions were as Table A.

Dragoons

In 1877 the dragoons not only fought like infantry but were dressed in very similar uniforms. They wore green tunics with the collars piped in the regimental colour, and green kepis. A green sash edged with the regimental colour was worn around the waist. Distinctions were as Table B.

Uhlans

The 14 uhlan regiments created towards the end of the Napoleonic wars were also destined to become dragoons in 1882. In 1877 the Russian uhlans wore what were essentially Napoleonic uniforms consisting of blue *kurtkas* with collars, lapels and cuffs in the regimental colour. Those uhlan regiments sent to the Balkans appear to have worn *furashkas* instead of the regulation *czapskas*. Distinctions were as Table C.

Table A: Hussar distinctions

Regiment	Attila	Kepi
1	pale blue	red
2	green	pale blue
3	pale blue	white
4	dark blue	yellow
5	black	red
6	dark blue	pale blue
7	pale blue	white
8	dark blue	yellow
9	green	red
10	pale blue	pale blue
11	dark blue	white
12	brown	yellow
13	pale blue	yellow
14	green	yellow

Loopings on the Attila were white for regiments 5, 6, 7, 8, 13 and 14; yellow for the others. The Guard hussars (still mounted exclusively on white horses) had not adopted Attilas, and retained their red dolmans and dark blue pelisses. They had red kepis and sabretaches; loopings were orange-yellow. The Grodno Hussar Regiment, also part of the Russian Guard, were similarly uniformed but could be distinguished by white loopings and a pale blue kepi.

Table B: Dragoon distinctions

Regiment	Collar	Collar patches	Cuffs
1	green	red	red
2	green	pink	pink
3	green	pale blue	pale blue
4	green	pale blue	pale blue
5	green	white	white
6	green	white	white
7	green	yellow	yellow
8	green	yellow	yellow
9	red	green	red
10	red	green	red
11	pale blue	green	pale blue
12	pale blue	green	pale blue
13	orange	green	orange
14	yellow	green	yellow
15	green	crimson	crimson
16	crimson	green	crimson
17	green	crimson	crimson
18	crimson	green	crimson

Buttons were yellow for odd-numbered regiments and white for even-numbered regiments, except for the 16th and 17th Dragoons which had yellow and white buttons respectively.

Mounted Russian officers lead their close-packed formations against the dug-in Turks. Pre-war Russian doctrine called for thin skirmish lines followed by shoulder-to-shoulder infantry companies. With only 10 or 20 per cent of an infantry regiment's rifles actually being fired during this primitive type of assault, the Russians' initial attacks broke down with heavy losses. (Author's Collection)

Table C: Uhlan distinctions

Regiment	Collar	Collar patches	Lapels, cuffs & czapska sides
1	blue	red	red
2	blue	pale blue	pale blue
3	blue	white	white
4	blue	yellow	yellow
5	blue	red	red
6	blue	pale blue	pale blue
7	blue	white	white
8	blue	yellow	white
9	red	blue	red
10	pale blue	blue	pale blue
11	white	blue	white
12	yellow	blue	yellow
13	yellow	—	yellow
14	pale blue	—	pale blue

Buttons were yellow for regiments 1, 2, 3, 4, 9, 10, 11 and 12; white for the others.

Cossacks

With the exception of the Caucasian Cossack regiments, the Cossacks looked similar to the line cavalry regiments. Although fur caps were supposed to be worn, many Cossacks wore their undress *furashkas* throughout the summer campaign in Bulgaria. Their uniform consisted of blue jacket and blue trousers with collar, piping, shoulder straps and cap bag in the regimental colour. The Little Russia and Orenburg Regiments wore green jackets and trousers instead. Regimental distinctions were as Table D.

Artillery

Russian field artillery had failed dismally in the Crimean War and, since Russia lacked the technology to produce rifled cannon, an entirely new range of bronze smoothbores had been introduced in the early 1860s. But although the Russian arsenals delivered over 1,100 new cannons in four years – as many guns as the Federal factories manufactured during the American Civil War – these were only a stop-gap. By 1867 Gadolin and Maevsky had perfected their system of casting rifled breechloading cannon from

The small town of Plevna became a household name in 1877 because of its strategic position commanding the road to the Balkan passes. The Turks entrenched themselves here, and threw back a succession of Russian assaults. (Author's Collection)

bronze. Other countries had tested bronze rifled cannon, but they were not widely adopted. American tests in the 1850s demonstrated that bronze rifling wore out very quickly – hence the decision to use bronze for smoothbore ordnance but iron for rifled cannon. Perhaps the Russians' secret was the parsimony of the War Ministry: Russian field guns were issued with only one full-charge round per year for training! In 1876 each battery was also allocated four shrapnel rounds per year.

Each Russian infantry division was supported by an artillery brigade of six eight-gun batteries: three of 4-pdr. guns and three of 9-pdr. guns. They actually fired shells weighing 12 pounds and 24 pounds

Table D: Cossack distinctions

Regiment	Collar	Piping	Shoulder straps	Girdle	Cap bag
Don	blue	red	blue	black	red
Black Sea	blue	red	blue	white	red
Astrakhan	blue	yellow	yellow	yellow	yellow
Little Russia	green	red	red	black	red
Azov	blue	white	blue	white	red
Danube	blue	red	blue	red	red
Ural	blue	pale blue	pale blue	pale blue	pale blue
Stavropol	red	blue	red	red	red
Mersherya	blue	blue	blue	black	pale blue
Orenburg	green	pale blue	pale blue	pale blue	red
Siberia	blue	blue	red	red	red
Tobolsk	red	blue	red	black	blue
Yeniseisk	red	blue	red	black	blue
Irkutsk	red	blue	red	black	blue
Sabaikal	red	blue	red	black	blue
Yakutsk	red	blue	red	black	blue
Tartar	red	blue	red	black	blue

The Caucasian regiments wore the *Cherkeska* – a collarless long coat with loops for rifle cartridges sewn into the front. The *Cherkeskas* were blue for the Caucasus, Kuban, Coper, Volga and Stavropol Regiments; brown for the Gor, Greben, Mosdak and Kisler Regiments. All wore fur caps. Cossack cavalry were armed with lances and *shashkas* – sabres without guards. Dismounted Cossacks (*plastuny*) wore the same uniform as their mounted comrades but were armed with rifles.

respectively; the Russians followed conventional European practice in naming a rifled gun after the weight of the round ball it would fire if it were a smoothbore. The 3.2-in. calibre 4-pdr. had an effective range of 2,500 metres and the 4.2-in. calibre 9-pdr. was considered effective at up to 3,200 metres. Both guns were outranged by the Krupp steel breechloaders in limited service with the Turkish army, but the Ottoman forces had fewer than 50 Krupp cannon available in 1877.

Four types of rounds were provided for the Russian field guns: high-explosive with percussion fuse; incendiary; time-fused shrapnel; and canister. The latter was distinctly inferior to the canister fired from earlier smoothbore guns, and at its effective range of 400 metres the gunners were sitting ducks for enemy infantry armed with Martini-Peabody rifles. The guns were mounted on robust metal carriages which survived the rigours of the campaign in Bulgaria with flying colours. Perhaps the only weakness of the system was the relatively small number of rounds in the limbers: 18 rounds for each 4-pdr. or 12 per 9-pdr. The rest of the ammunition was carried in ammunition wagons, two per 4-pdr. gun and three per 9-pdr.

In 1877 there were five Guard, 21 line and 21 Cossack horse artillery batteries, each consisting of six 4-pdr. guns. Each cavalry division had two batteries attached; and the Don Cossacks were also supported by two batteries of eight 3-pdr. mountain guns. Also cast in bronze, these could be drawn by a single horse and had a range of 1,400 metres. Widely used in the Caucasian campaigns, the mountain guns proved very useful in the Balkan mountains. The

Osman Pasha became a national hero for defending Plevna. He pleaded with Constantinople for permission to withdraw once the Russians were able to encircle him, but the Sultan's War Council refused. (Author's Collection)

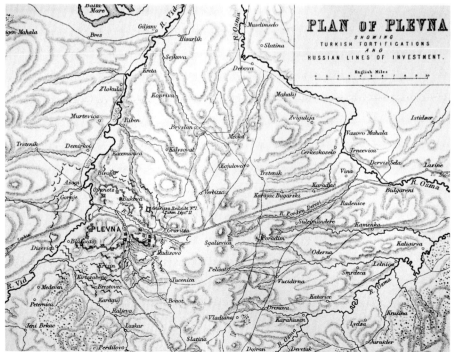

Left: The Russians never completely invested the sprawling Turkish defences of Plevna until late in October; before that stage the Turks were able to keep open their communications with Constantinople. (Author's Collection)

1: Russian Line Infantryman
2: Russian Line Infantryman,
   summer dress, Bulgaria, 1877
3: Russian Infantry Colonel

A

1: Russian Guards Infantry
2: Russian Guardsman, winter dress, January 1878
3: Cossack

B

1: Russian Dragoon
2: Lieutenant Dubasoff, Russian Navy
3: Russian Infantry Drummer

C

1: Russian Field Artilleryman
2: General Mikhail Skoboleff
3: Volunteer Bulgarian Legion

D

1: Turkish Regular Infantryman
2: Turkish Light Infantryman
3: Turkish Reservist

E

1: Turkish Artilleryman
2: Lieutenant-general
   Valentine Baker Pasha
3: Turkish Regular Cavalryman

F

1: Bashi-Bazouk
2: Egyptian Infantryman
3: Romanian Chasseur

1: Romanian Line Infantryman
2: Romanian Dorobantzi Infantryman
3: Roshiori Regular Cavalryman

H

Turkestan and Siberian artillery brigades had a battery of mountain guns instead of one of their 4-pdr. batteries.

The full strength of artillery batteries was:

4-pdr. foot	6 officers, 256 men, 169 horses, 16 wagons.
4-pdr. horse	6 officers, 253 men, 241 horses, 16 wagons.
9-pdr.	6 officers, 317 men, 223 horses, 24 wagons.

All batteries also included two store wagons, three general service wagons, one implement wagon and a field forge. The wagons were of relatively light construction and were pulled by three horses abreast. In column of route a light battery occupied 460 paces and a heavy battery 570 paces.

Uniforms

Since 1801 the Russian field artillery uniform had resembled that of the infantry. In 1877 the gunners wore a green uniform in the infantry style but with black distinctions instead of red. They wore a kepi like that of the line infantry, and were issued with the same hooded greatcoat, but on campaign the gunners were also seen wearing *furashka*.

THE TURKISH ARMY

The Tsar's decision to declare war on Turkey caught his own army in the middle of a reorganization inspired by the Prussian military system. The Turkish army had adopted some Prussian ideas too, but its reorganization was completed, and by the spring of 1877 most of the army was already in the field. For all its shortcomings, the Turkish army had not been better prepared for war since the 17th century.

Since 1874 the Turkish army had been recruited by conscription. This applied only to Muslim inhabitants of the empire; despite an 1856 decision to recruit men of all religions, in 1877 non-Muslims were still left out of the army and paid a tax instead. There were some exceptions: the citizens of Constan-

Turkish artillerymen fire their Krupp steel cannon against dense masses of Russian infantry at Plevna. The Krupp outranged the rifled bronze pieces used by the Russians, but the Turkish guns were heavily outnumbered and their horse-teams were chronically understrength. (Author's Collection)

tinople and nomad tribes did not have to serve, and men of the most modest means could buy themselves out after three months' service.

The Ottoman Empire was divided into seven territorially based army corps. The 1st (Guards) Corps was based at Constantinople; the 2nd (Danube) Corps at Shumla; the 3rd (Roumelia) Corps at Monastir; the 4th (Anatolia) Corps at Erzerzoum; the 5th (Syria) Corps at Damascus; the 6th (Iraq) Corps at Baghdad; and the 7th (Arabia) Corps in the Yemen. The numerical strength and military value of these corps varied considerably. It is not surprising to learn that the Baghdad-based 6th Corps only managed to send a weak division to take part in the fighting, and that only towards the end of the war.

Each corps district provided a *Nizam* or active army in which conscripts served for four years in the infantry or five in the cavalry or artillery. Regardless of the official procedure in Constantinople, conscripts were often obtained by methods remarkably similar to those used by Royal Navy press-gangs during the Napoleonic wars. Villages would be surrounded during the night and, before dawn, enough young men to fill the quota would be rousted from their homes by soldiers.

After serving his time in the *Nizam* a Turkish soldier passed into the *Ihtiat* (first reserve), for two years if in the infantry or one if cavalry or artillery. After that he passed into the *Redif* (second reserve) for another eight years. The *Redif* was subdivided

into four classes; the first class was made up of former *Nizam* troops; the third class comprised men who had escaped conscription. After four years in the *Redif* the first class became the second class and the third class became the fourth class. Since reserve battalions were recruited entirely from men of the same class, those from the third and fourth classes of *Redif* were of little fighting value. The *Redif* battalions were supposed to be organized and equipped exactly like the *Nizam*, but they tended to have older weapons. In peacetime they had no officers and were rarely at full strength; in wartime NCOs from the *Nizam* were often promoted to become officers in *Redif* battalions.

After a soldier had completed his spell in the *Nizam*, *Ihtiat* and *Redif* he was still liable for duty: he joined the *Moustafiz* or territorial militia. By the time a man entered the *Moustafiz* he was about 35 years old. When it was called up in 1877 the ranks of the *Moustafiz* were swelled by large numbers of untrained civilian volunteers.

In the winter of 1875, as the fighting against the rebels in Herzegovina intensified, the Turks called up the *Ihtiat* and the first class of *Redif*; the second class was called up in 1876 on the outbreak of war with Serbia and Montenegro; and the third division followed suit in November when Russia mobilized troops in Bessarabia. The progressive mobilization of Turkey's military strength placed the Ottoman Empire in an unusually strong position. Had the reserv-

Osman Pasha's army at Plevna capitulated in December 1877 after an attempted break-out collapsed in the face of concentrated Russian artillery fire. The captured Turkish soldiers were then subjected to a traditional death-march through the winter. Few ever returned home. (Author's Collection)

ists not already been in the field in April 1877, the original Russian campaign might well have delivered the victory Gen. Obruchoff promised.

In the spring of 1877 the Ottoman army was estimated to have 150,000 *Nizam*, 190,000 *Redif* and 300,000 *Moustafiz*, but none of the classes had been maintained at full strength. The army was organized as follows:

First Corps (Constantinople)

Infantry: Seven line regiments (21 bns.)
Seven rifle battalions
Cavalry: Five line regiments
One Cossack brigade (two regts. of four sqns.)
Artillery: Nine field and three horse batteries
One *Ihtiat* regiment (twelve field batteries and one mountain battery)
Engineers: One sapper company
Eight companies of engineers
One company of artificers

Second Corps (Danube)

Infantry: Six line regiments (18 bns.)
Six rifle battalions
Danube frontier regiment (three bns.)
Cavalry: Four regiments
Artillery: One line regiment (12 batteries)
Engineers: One sapper company

Third Corps (Roumelia)

Infantry: Seven line regiments (21 bns.)
Seven rifle battalions
Bosnian brigade (six bns.)
Frontier regiment on Greek border (three bns.)
Frontier regiment on Bosnian border (four bns.)
Frontier battalion (Niksich)
Austro-Herzegovinian battalion
Cavalry: Four regiments
Artillery: One line regiment (12 batteries)
Three mountain batteries in Herzegovina
Engineers: One sapper company

Fourth Corps (Anatolia)

Infantry: Five line regiments (15 bns.)

One regiment of one battalion
Six rifle battalions
Cavalry: Three line regiments
Artillery: One line regiment (12 batteries)
Engineers: One sapper company

Fifth Corps (Syria)

Infantry: Seven line regiments (21 bns.)
Seven rifle battalions
Cavalry: Four line regiments
Artillery: One line regiment (12 batteries)
Engineers: One sapper company

Sixth Corps (Baghdad)

Infantry: Six line regiments (18 bns.)
Six rifle battalions
Cavalry: Two line regiments
Artillery: One regiment (9 batteries)

Seventh Corps (Yemen)

Infantry: Five line regiments (15 bns.)
Five rifle battalions
Cavalry: One squadron Circassians
Artillery: One regiment (six batteries)

Infantry organization

Turkish infantry regiments usually comprised three battalions, but they were administrative units only. On the battlefield battalions were grouped together for combat without any regard for regimental structure. It was standard practice to mix battalions from different corps, let alone regiments, into ad hoc tactical units. This haphazard system led to considerable confusion during the fighting – and afterwards, when participants tried to tell their story. In 1878 the infantry battalions were consolidated into permanent regiments with consecutive numbering.

A full-strength infantry battalion consisted of 819 officers and men, organized into eight companies and commanded by a colonel (*Bimbashi*). Each 102-man company had two lieutenants, two sergeants and two corporals. Rifle (*Tallia*) battalions were supposed to have 828 men, the extra personnel supplying the crews for two Whitworth mountain guns. However, by 1877, many regular battalions involved in the earlier Balkan campaigns only mustered about 500 men. Many battalion commanders reorganized their depleted units into four companies; they were short of officers, and the existing companies were too weak to serve any practical value.

During the war the Turks tended to form new recruits into fresh battalions rather than sending them as replacements to existing units. The regular battalions dwindled while large, untrained and ill-disciplined battalions of recruits were sent into action.

Armament

The Turks accorded top priority to the purchase of modern weaponry, continuing to pay American and European arms companies in gold while the Empire declared itself bankrupt in 1875. By 1877 the majority of Turkish infantry battalions were armed with the Martini-Peabody rifle. Sighted to 1,800 yards, this single-shot breechloader was chambered for the 11.43×55mm rimmed cartridge (.45 Peabody), which fired a 486-grain lead bullet with a muzzle velocity of 1,265 feet per second. Under combat conditions this was almost as accurate as the smokeless powder weapons in service by the end of the century, and it entirely outclassed the Russian Krnk. Valentine Baker Pasha recalled one Russian infantry attack: 'On arriving within 800 yards of the Turkish line, they halted and opened fire. The Krnk rifle with which they were armed was miserably ineffective at this range, while even at this distance, the answering fire of the Turks with the Henry-Martini [*sic*] told heavily.' Baker should not be censured for confusing the Martini-Peabody with the Martini-Henry; the Turkish rifle looked almost identical to that in service with the British army. The ammunition was mostly imported from the USA; some accidents occurred when proud primers were detonated prematurely by the closing of the breech, but, unlike the damage-prone rolled types manufactured at Woolwich for the British army, the cartridge cases were solid brass.

The rest of the Turkish infantry were armed with British Snider rifles; chambered for the .577 rimmed cartridge, these were Enfield rifled muskets converted to breechloaders. Replaced in the British army by the Martini-Henry, the Snider was a robust weapon if not as accurate as its successor. Sighted to 950 yards, it was not significantly superior to the Krnk.

Detail of the breech of an American-made Martini-Peabody rifle, the most common weapon of the Turkish infantry. The ammunition was imported from the USA as well – paid for in gold, while the Ottoman Empire defaulted on its foreign loans. (Author's Collection)

Above: The Russians made up for the inauspicious start to their campaign in the Caucasus by the storming of the fortress of Kars on the night of 17–18 November. They drew off the Turkish reserves with an elaborate deception plan, and stormed the key Turkish redoubts after several hours' desperate fighting. (Author's Collection)

Uniform

Until the Napoleonic Wars the soldiers of the Ottoman Empire continued to wear traditional dress that harked back to the glory days of the 16th century. The first attempt to introduce European-style uniforms sparked a mutiny in 1807: Sultan Selim III was deposed, his political and military reforms were overturned, and the officials who had tried to implement them were torn to pieces in the streets of Constantinople.

The next Sultan to introduce European dress met with more success. Mahmud II ordered the Janissaries to adopt a modern uniform in 1826, and this time he was ready for the revolt that followed; the Sultan had the religious leadership on his side, the mobs failed to materialize, and the mutinous soldiers were suppressed with draconian efficiency.

Mahmud II introduced a dark blue uniform that would be worn by the Turkish infantry from the 1828–9 Russo-Turkish War until 1909, when it was replaced by a khaki service dress. The exact cut of the uniform varied over the years, retaining short jackets and baggy Zouave trousers until the 1890s when a more Germanic style was adopted. In 1877 Turkish infantrymen wore a plain blue tunic and blue trousers. Footwear consisted of top-boots, or untanned leather shoes with gaiters that reached almost to the knee. William von Herbert described the boots issued to his battalion as 'execrable', but Russian infantrymen frequently helped themselves to the boots of Turkish casualties during the fighting at Shipka in January 1878, by which date they had worn out their own by hard marching through the mountains.

Overcoats were issued in both grey and dark blue and were supplied with a hood similar to that worn by the Russian infantry. Facings and shoulder straps were red for line infantry and green for the light infantry battalions. All ranks wore a red fez; this afforded no protection from the weather, and many soldiers wrapped cloth turbans around them. Baker Pasha and his staff wore white turbans, but a correspondent in Armenia observed 'rags of clothes of any and every colour wrapped around the universal fez'.

Baker encountered a volunteer battalion clothed and equipped by a patriotic Armenian of Constantinople, 'dressed entirely in a uniform of the brown Bulgarian cloth'. There may well have been other units wearing improvised uniforms, as the supply of clothing to the army was not one of the Sultan's top priorities in the 1870s. Many units had not received new uniforms for several years; jackets and trousers that were supposed to be blue ranged from dark blue to greenish grey, with every shade in between. A German officer serving with the Russians described the Turks captured at Shipka as 'mostly in rags and tatters, looking more like brigands than soldiers'.

The infantryman's equipment consisted of an ammunition pouch for 80 rounds, a water bottle and a canvas haversack. Many troops wound red sashes around their waists and stuffed extra packs of cartridges into them.

The Romanian army was led into battle by King Charles I, a German prince and former officer cadet in the Prussian army. Here Romanian infantry storm the Turkish Danube fortress of Rahova. They wear Russian-style greatcoats, kepis, and carry Peabody rifles. (Author's Collection)

Cavalry organization

Regular cavalry regiments consisted of 131 officers, NCOs and staff and 831 men. They were divided into six squadrons, each with a peacetime strength of 90 officers and men, expanding to 152 in wartime. On paper there were 158 squadrons with a total strength of 20,540 men, plus about 10,000 irregular horse, available in 1877. The regular cavalry units were hampered by poor quality horses and bad leadership, rendering their impact on the campaign negligible. Normally found well to the rear of the battlefield, they had little thought of scouting, and if they did encounter the Russians they tended to blaze away with their carbines at maximum range.

The cavalry uniform was almost identical to that of the infantry. Wearing a dark blue jacket and trousers tucked into boots, the regular cavalrymen wore a sheepskin cap instead of a fez. The irregular cavalry wore the most exotic costumes of the campaign: short waistcoats, baggy trousers and turbans.

Armament

Turkish cavalry were equipped with the famous Winchester '73 carbine, a sword and a revolver. Four squadrons of the Guards cavalry regiments were equipped with lances (the other two 'flank' squadrons retaining carbines). The Turks bought several types of Winchester including the 12-shot carbine and the 15-shot rifle, which had barrel lengths of 20 and 24 inches respectively; but they ordered enough of the fully stocked 30in.-barrel rifles for them to become known in America as the 'Turkish musket'. The tubular magazine was in proportion to the long barrel and held no fewer than 17 rounds. A determined body of Turks armed with Winchesters could achieve a devastating rate of fire – until they had to reload their magazines. Circassian irregulars seem to have been almost uniformly equipped with Winchesters, several commentators using the expression 'Circassian carbine' when referring to them. Yet

Russian lancers overrun a Turkish strongpoint in a fanciful illustration depicting the final battles south of the Balkans. Russian accounts of the war exaggerated these text-book victories – which did involve cavalry attacks on the beaten foe – but played down the disasters at Plevna. (Author's Collection)

technology can only achieve so much – there were few determined bodies of Turks so armed. The irregular cavalry were little more than bandits, hovering on the fringes of the battlefields in search of loot.

Artillery

The artillery was organized into batteries of six guns, commanded by a captain and consisting of 132–164 men. These were grouped together into battalions of four field batteries, one horse battery and one Gatling battery. Three such battalions constituted an artillery regiment, but in practice the Turkish artillery was very thinly spread. The quality of their draft horses was never high, and the training of many officers and men left much to be desired.

Turkish horse artillery batteries and two battalions of field artillery were equipped with 4-pdr. and 6-pdr. Krupp steel breechloaders. These outranged the Russian artillery, but the Turks were handicapped by their lack of horses – many teams were incomplete – and a shortage of ammunition wagons. There were supposed to be six per battery, but few even started the war at full establishment. Osman Pasha's army at Plevna had some of the Krupp guns,

and others were present with Suleiman's forces south of the Balkan mountains. Perversely, it was a battery of Turkish Krupp cannon captured by the Russians that had the greatest impact on a Balkan battlefield. When the Turks abandoned the Shipka Pass they left a battery behind in one of their redoubts. Rechristened Fort St. Nicholas, this position played a key role in defeating the desperate counter-attacks launched by Suleiman's army. In an impressive demonstration of the power of breechloading artillery, the gunners maintained a heavy fire even when Turkish infantry had advanced to within 200 yards of the earthworks. Dug in on a reverse slope, they were effectively sheltered from the Turkish rifle fire.

The remainder of the Turkish artillery were armed, like the Russians, with bronze breechloaders built after the Krupp pattern. They did not wear as

Russian infantrymen with their hoods worn over their greatcoats and knapsacks on their backs. They are supposed to be examining grim evidence of Turkish atrocities. The worst outrages of the war were perpetrated by Turkish irregulars, but elements of the local Christian population also massacred their Muslim neighbours in a foretaste of 20th-century 'ethnic cleansing'. (Author's Collection)

The Russians' bronze breechloading cannon were mounted on robust metal carriages. However, the pre-war practice allowance of just one live round per gun per year seriously handicapped the gunners' performance in 1877. (Author's Collection)

well as steel cannon, and when their breeches showed signs of damage the Turks strengthened them with iron bands. Of course, there was nothing that could be done about the rifling, which was rapidly worn away, degrading accuracy and increasing the chance of premature detonation.

The Russian army had flirted briefly with US-made Gatling guns in the 1870s before consigning them to fortress defence. In 1877, however, the Turks still had some 200 Austrian-made 10-barrel Gatling guns, chambered for the .58 calibre Snider cartridge. They were organized into six-gun batteries and employed alongside the field guns. However, contemporary accounts of the war are not overburdened with descriptions of Turkish Gatlings in action.

Uniforms

The Turkish artillery wore blue jackets braided with red; blue trousers were tucked into top-boots, and headgear was either a fez like that of the infantry or a *kalpak* as worn by the cavalry. A cavalry-type hat may have been worn to distinguish horse artillery

gunners from the field artillery, but as horses and personnel were soon mixed indiscriminately it had little practical effect. Gunners were issued with cavalry swords and revolvers as sidearms.

THE PLATES

A1: Russian line infantryman

The French-style uniform introduced in 1855 was distinctly unfashionable by 1877. The explosion of 'Pan-Slav' sentiment spurred the adoption of more 'Russian' uniforms, and during the 1870s the Guards, Rifles and Grenadiers abandoned the uniform introduced in the wake of the Crimean War. However, the initial invasion of Bulgaria was undertaken by seven regular army corps, largely dressed in regulation uniform. The single-breasted green jacket was worn with green trousers in winter and white ones for summer – most contemporary illustrations show line infantry dressed in their white trousers for the crossing of the Danube in April. Although some line infantry regiments had received Berdan rifles by

1877 the majority of line divisions deployed to Bulgaria were still armed with Krnk rifles. This private has swung open the heavy brass 'trap door' to insert a fresh cartridge into the breech; note that the hammer has to be at half-cock to permit the breech to open. To fire, he will swing the 'trap door' shut, pressing down until it clicks into place; pull the hammer back to full cock; and pull the trigger.

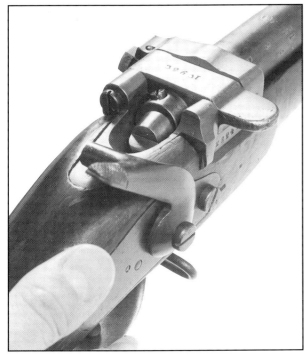

Detail of the breech of the Russian Krnk rifle. To load, the hammer is pulled back to half-cock and the 'trapdoor' swung open. The sights were described by a contemporary as designed solely to get around existing patents. Badly balanced and not particularly accurate, the Krnk is extremely robust – a classic Russian 'soldier-proof' weapon. (Author's Collection)

A2: Russian line infantry, summer dress; Bulgaria, 1877

The trend towards more Slavic uniforms was led by the soldiers fighting Russia's colonial wars across central Asia. They adopted a loose-fitting white blouse which was to become the model for subsequent Russian, and later Soviet uniforms. By the summer of 1877 this was no longer the exclusive preserve of the Caucasian Corps or the Rifle regiments, also being worn by line infantry regiments. The troops copied the central Asian practice of fitting their kepis with Havelocks to protect the backs of their necks from the sun. This line infantryman is armed with a Krnk rifle, and in accordance with the tactical doctrine of the time he keeps his bayonet fixed. The cult of the bayonet was followed with slavish devotion by pre-war Russian theorists, and Russian infantry frequently assaulted Turkish positions in close formations with little suppressive fire.

A3: Russian infantry colonel

Russian officers wore a similar uniform to that of their men – the line colonels in regulation dress, those of the Guards and other fashionable units going to war in *gimnasterkas* with *furashkas* instead of kepis. All officers were issued with the 1855-pattern officers' greatcoat, which was often worn like a cloak. Subalterns had a small knapsack for their personal kit. More senior officers usually rode into action,

often paying the price of presenting such a spectacular target. Even if they dismounted, the tendency of Russian officers to have much cleaner and whiter jackets than their men had not gone unnoticed by the Turks. The summer battles cost the Russian army so many infantry officers that cavalry officers had to be drafted into infantry units to replace them. Officers were armed with swords and Smith & Wesson 'Russian' .44 single-action revolvers.

B1: Russian Guardsman

The Russian Guard was organized, dressed and armed differently from the line infantry: Guard and Grenadier battalions were divided into four companies rather than five, and wore a green tunic with white piping rather than red. The regulation kepi was replaced by a white *furashka*, and the Krnk rifle by the new Berdan – mostly Berdan Mk IIs. This Guardsman has acquired an 1834 pattern sappers' bayonet for use as a general-purpose field knife. His bayonet, in accordance with regulations, remains permanently fixed to his rifle. The Guard included three infantry divisions in 1877, made up of 16 battalions rather than the 12 of a line division: divisions consisted of two brigades each of two four-battalion regiments. Guards divisions included a Rifle brigade, and a brigade of field artillery: six eight-gun batteries equipped exclusively with 9-pdr. guns. At full establishment, the Imperial Guard provided the Tsar with 49,000 infantry, 7,500 cavalry, 144 field guns and 36 horse guns.

B2: Russian Guardsman, January 1878

The 1st Guards Division learned some harsh lessons in October, suffering unnecessarily heavy losses attacking Turkish outposts near Plevna. After this brutal introduction to the effects of modern small arms fire the Guards performed well – they took part in the epic march over the Balkan passes in December, and in the final battles south of the mountains. The Guards Jägers stormed the bridge over the River Isker, opening the way to Sophia. The Preobrajensky and Semenovsky Guard Infantry Regiments and the Guard Lancers led the advance into the city – the first Christian army to enter it since 1434. This Guardsman wears the earth-brown greatcoat virtually universal in the Russian army at that time. With his hood up, he is, in silhouette, little different from a Turkish soldier. Note the cloth wrapped around the bolt of his Berdan rifle to keep snow and ice out of the action.

B3: Cossack

This Cossack wears the traditional fur hat that was to remain part of the Cossack uniform until after World War II. In 1877 officers and men of the Cossack regiments often wore white *furashkas* instead, particularly during the summer campaign. Increasingly used for internal security duties as well as to supplement the regular cavalry in wartime, the Cossacks were regarded as an anachronism by many influential Russian officers. But Russia needed more cavalry – particularly after studies of the Franco-Prussian War

Russian gunners haul a pack gun on a sled during the crossing of the Balkans. The Russians lost more men to the appalling weather conditions than to Turkish action, and took the gamble of a winter attack because of the growing threat of Great Power intervention. (Author's Collection)

argued the need for good screening and reconnaissance. From 1874 the Cossacks began to be incorporated into the regular cavalry divisions. Armed and equipped in a similar manner to the regulars, they provided over 140,000 officers and men during the war – nearly three-quarters of the Russian cavalry. However, dressing them in modern uniforms and issuing carbines did not convert an essentially tribal militia into regular cavalry. They were not capable of effective action on the battlefield, mounted or on foot, nor was their scouting particularly effective. The fact that the Turks were able to keep communications with Plevna open for so long, and that the Russians were usually ignorant of Turkish dispositions, exposed the Cossacks' limitations.

C1: Russian Dragoon

While most European cavalry still clung to the idea of shock action, the Russian dragoons were training for dismounted combat. In 1877 the dragoons were theoretically equipped with a carbine version of the Berdan II, but some regiments went to war still armed with the Krnk. Dressed like the infantry, and not shy of fighting on foot, the Russian dragoons proved rather more valuable than the hussars and uhlans – who remained hostages to the Napoleonic tradition. After the war Gourko's staff officer, Gen. Sukotin, managed to reorganize all hussar and uhlan regiments into dragoons, and to organize an imposing cavalry corps in the Warsaw Military district, ready to mount a strategic raid into Germany or Austria-Hungary in the event of war. Dressed very like the infantry, the dragoons' only serious shortcoming was their ammunition allowance of 20 rounds per man – standard for all Russian cavalry. They were not able to sustain a prolonged firefight with enemy infantry.

C2: Lieutenant Dubasoff, Russian Navy

The Turkish squadron of modern ironclads proved singularly ineffective in contesting the Russian crossing of the Danube. Although commanded by an ex-Royal Navy captain, the Turkish warships were poorly manned and timidly captained. While the Turks played a strong hand badly, the Russians exploited every resource at their disposal. One ironclad, the *Lufti Djelil*, was destroyed by two 8-in. siege guns when a shell dropped through the deck and penetrated the magazine. Then, in a daring attack

Russian infantry march through the frozen Balkan mountains. Temperatures dipped well below zero, but the offensive caught the Turks by surprise and *the Russians were able to capture Sophia and Adrianople in quick succession. (Author's Collection)*

that was to be reported around the world, Lts. Dubasoff and Shestakoff attacked the river monitor *Seife* during the early hours of 26 May. Each commanding a black-painted steam launch armed with two spar torpedoes, they managed to place their charges under the stern of the monitor. The explosion sent it to the bottom of the Danube, and both boats escaped in a hail of fire from the sinking monitor and other Turkish warships.

C3: Russian infantry drummer

Apart from the distinctive shoulder wings, the drummers of the infantry regiments wore the standard infantry uniform. At full wartime establishments each infantry battalion included three buglers and three drummers.

D1: Russian field artilleryman

Russian cannon had metal carriages robust enough to survive crossing the Balkan mountains by the roughest of trails; for the Russian gunners, however, it was a grim struggle against the elements. This gunner wears full winter kit, with his hands protected by mittens to stop them freezing to the metal. Underneath his greatcoat he wears a green tunic and trousers tucked into top-boots. Gunners wore a kepi similar to that of the infantry.

D2: General Skoboleff

Gen. Mikhail Skoboleff is seen here leading his men into the Turkish redoubt at Plevna, after he had his fifth horse killed under him; his sword was broken by the same shell, and he led the final charge with just the broken blade. The most controversial Russian officer of the war, 33-year-old Skoboleff cut a dashing figure with his white uniform, white horse, and extravagant blond whiskers. He had a charmed life – leading the assault in person he attracted a hail of fire, but escaped without injury; all his accompanying staff officers were shot. Skoboleff is idolized in many contemporary accounts of the campaign and was often depicted as the only competent commander on the Russian side. In fact he was one of the first generals in any army to exploit the new-found power of the 19th-century newspaper business. He courted correspondents, especially British journalists, handing out medals and such war trophies as the captured swords of Turkish officers. He was popular with his men – perhaps they had a share in the Turkish military pay chest secured by his troops at Shipka and almost emptied before it reached the Russian field treasury. They also followed his orders not to take prisoners. Like his father, Skoboleff made a fortune serving in the army in central Asia. Aristocratic officers like Prince Mirsky described him as 'an officer with whom, in peace, no-one would shake hands.'

D3: Volunteer, Bulgarian Legion

The Bulgarian independence movement had an uneasy relationship with Tsarist Russia. It needed Russian assistance to escape from Turkish rule, but few Bulgarians wished to swap the Sultan for the Tsar. By the 1870s the children of wealthier Bulgarian families were often educated in Russia (where some apparently stayed to form a core of reliable men in the Moscow secret police). In 1877 the volunteers were organized into six rifle battalions, equipped like those of the Imperial army and armed similarly with Berdan rifles. They fought with distinction, forming part of Gourko's column which seized the Shipka Pass. They suffered grievous losses in the subsequent Turkish assaults on the position, but held their ground with the same dogged endurance displayed by their Russian allies. The Bulgarians had wished to serve under their own officers, but the Tsar refused to countenance the creation of a semi-independent force; the officers were all seconded from the Russian army.

E1: Turkish regular infantryman

This private soldier (*Nefer*) belongs to one of the Ottoman Empire's 168 active battalions or *Nizamié*. These regular troops were the backbone of the Turkish defence in 1877. The red fez with its blue tassel was worn throughout the army. Line infantrymen wore blue jackets and vests which were piped yellow for the first regiment of each corps, and red for all other regiments. They wore baggy blue trousers either tucked into top-boots or with gaiters and shoes. Their blue or grey overcoats were hooded. In the European corps districts the standard of clothing was generally high except for the government-issue boots. Military equipment consisted of a leather cartridge box holding 80 rounds, a water bottle and a canvas haversack. This soldier sports a red sash around his waist, popular with the regular troops and often used to carry extra ammunition (some had pouches specially sewn in). He is armed with the excellent Martini-Peabody rifle made by the Providence Tool Company, Rhode Island, of which Turkey ordered 400,000. Almost indistinguishable from the British Martini-Henry, in the hands of a competent shot it was extremely accurate; it was superior to the Russian Berdan, and vastly outclassed the Krnk rifle issued to many Russian line regiments. The Turks frequently brought the Russians under effective fire at 1,000 metres.

E2: Turkish light infantryman

In the Turkish standing army there was one battalion of *Tallié* (Rifles) per three-battalion regiment of line infantry. They were distinguished from the line troops by green facings instead of red. In theory, each battalion was provided with two Whitworth-system breechloading mountain guns, each carried on a pair

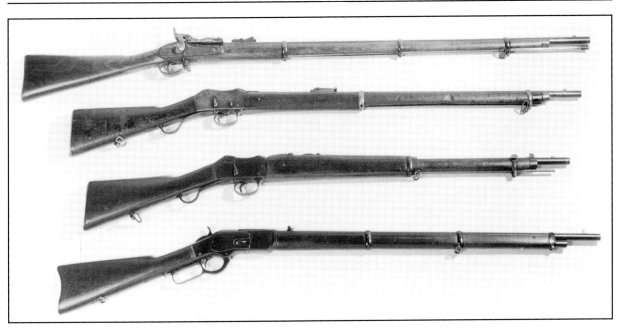

Turkish rifles from the Russo-Turkish War belonging to the Pattern Room Collection. From the top: British Snider; Martini-Peabody rifle; *Martini-Peabody carbine; Winchester Model 73 'Turkish musket' or military rifle. (Author's Collection)*

of packhorses; these weapons do not figure prominently in accounts of the fighting, however, and the training and equipment of the *Tallié* were otherwise indistinguishable from the rest of the Turkish foot soldiers, apart from having sword bayonets.

E3: Turkish reservist

After serving two years in a *Nizam* battalion, a Turkish regular passed to the *Ihtihat* (first reserve) for a further two years, and was then transferred to the *Redif* (second reserve) for six years. On mobilization, the *Redif* provided 24 battalions to the first five Turkish corps. In 1877 the reservists of the *Ihtihat* and *Redif* had already been recalled to the colours for the war with Serbia and Montenegro and counter-insurgency operations in Bulgaria. Their uniforms were the same as those of regular troops, but most reservists were armed with older Snider rifles acquired from the British from 1874 onwards. Sighted to 950 yards and firing a rimmed .577 cartridge, these were inferior to the Berdan but still a match for the Krnk. This reservist wears a uniform only recently issued, and thus presents a rather smarter appearance than his regular comrades, whose last uniform issue was anything up to five years before.

F1: Turkish infantry (winter dress)

The Turkish army suffered severely in the winter campaign; the troops defending the Balkan mountains had to survive temperatures of below 3° Fahrenheit. The regulation greatcoat was well made and hard wearing, with its hood a particularly welcome feature. However, Turkish soldiers were often let down by their poor quality boots, and many resorted to sheepskin sandals or other improvised kit during the winter months.

F2: Lieutenant-General Valentine Baker Pasha

Brother of the celebrated Nile explorer Sir Samuel Baker, Valentine was the former commanding officer of the 10th Hussars. Forced to resign after being convicted on a dubious charge of indecently assaulting a young woman on a train (being a close friend of the notorious Prince of Wales had not helped his defence), Baker joined the Turkish army. There were many other European officers serving the Porte at that time; senior ranks included Hobart Pasha, second son of the Duke of Buckingham and ex-captain RN, who commanded the navy. Mehemet Ali, christened Jules Détroit, was a German from Magdeburg (descended from a Huguenot family) who worked his way up from subaltern to general. Baker served under Mehemet Ali in eastern Bulgaria, distinguish-

Detail of the lock of an 1862 British Snider rifle supplied to the Turkish army. The breach opened sideways, as did that of the Russian Krnk rifle, but the Snider was the better weapon. Britain exported large quantities of Sniders after their replacement by the Martini-Henry in British service. (Author's Collection)

ing himself in the rearguard actions of the subsequent winter campaign. After the war he served in the Egyptian forces during the Mahdist rebellion, and was favoured to take command of the reorganized Egyptian army until Queen Victoria heard of the suggestion and forbade it. (His daughter was later courted by Kitchener; her tragic death in Cairo was to leave him a bitter man.) Baker is seen here in the uniform of a Turkish lieutenant-general. He and his staff copied the unofficial practice of the soldiers in wrapping a cloth turban around the fez to shade their eyes from the sun.

F3: Turkish regular cavalryman

Dressed the same as the infantry apart from the sheepskin cap and untanned leather boots, the Turkish regular cavalry were equipped with sabres, revolvers and Model 1873 Winchester carbines. A British observer, Lt.-Col. Fife-Cookson, dismissed the Winchester as 'a mere toy, as can be seen by looking at one of the cartridges, which is little longer than that of a revolver. This weapon had only a short effective range, and of course was not to be compared

to the Henry-Martini carbine.' Some of the Turkish cavalry did have Martini-Peabody carbines; but whatever weapon they had, they tended to rely on their firearms rather than cold steel. Commanded by undistinguished officers, they usually skirmished at long range rather than seriously challenging the Russian cavalry. They were handicapped by the poor quality of their horses, which deteriorated further as the war continued and Turkish supply and remount arrangements collapsed altogether.

G1: Bashi-Bazouk

Described by even the most charitable observers as 'a group of undisciplined brigands', these were tribal forces employed by the Ottoman Empire to suppress revolts from the Danube to the Euphrates. The term *Bashi-Bazouk* meant civilian volunteer; but while many battalions of volunteer infantry came into being at Constantinople and other major Turkish cities, the *Bashi-Bazouks* came from different stock. According to another British officer, they were 'men gathered together from the remotest parts of the Turkish Empire – Arnauts from Albania, Greek renegades from Thessaly, the scum of Smyrna and Alexandria, robbers from the Lebanon, Bedouins from Palmyra, Zeibecks from Vidin and last, and yet first in blood-thirstiness and insatiable love of rapine, the Circassians and Georgians'. The Circassian tribes had been driven out of the Caucasus by the Russians only a generation before, and the Turkish authorities had quartered them in Bulgaria to suppress the Christian rebels. *Bashi-Bazouks* were responsible for numerous atrocities against Russian wounded, prisoners-of-war and Bulgarian civilians. Baker Pasha recorded having some of them bastinadoed, but they generally went unpunished.

G2: Egyptian infantryman

Organized and equipped along European lines, the Egyptian army created by Mohammed Ali was far superior to the unreformed Turkish forces of the early 19th century. It was an Egyptian army, backed by an Egyptian fleet, which all but extinguished the Greek rebellion, succeeding where the Turks had failed. When Constantinople challenged Egyptian control of Syria and the Lebanon in the 1830s, the Turkish army was decisively defeated – despite having a certain Major Helmuth von Moltke as its military advisor. By 1877 the tables had turned when Egypt supplied a division of Sudanese soldiers under Oxford-educated Prince Hassan. Better equipped than the Turks, and led by cultured officers fluent in European languages, the Egyptian contingent dug magnificent earthworks to defend its positions. However, the division proved as ineffective on the offensive as most Turkish troops in eastern Bulgaria – largely due to appalling staff work. They wore the dark blue Egyptian winter service dress and were armed with Remington rifles. A French correspondent who witnessed their arrival at Varna described them as 'nice little soldiers with chocolate faces and uniforms of dark blue cloth; they were so pretty, so prim, so well dressed, that one began to hope it would not rain for fear they should melt away. One could have sworn that they had all come out of boxes of toys from the Black Forest.'

G3: Romanian chasseur

The Romanian chasseur battalions wore an unusual uniform consisting of a brown double-breasted coat with green cuffs, dark grey trousers, and a round black leather hat not unlike a bowler. The coat and trousers were piped green. In full dress, the hat was decorated with a green cock's feather and the Romanian cockade. Their leather equipment was black, and they were armed with Peabody rifles.

H1: Romanian line infantryman

The uniform of the Romanian army dated from 1861, when Wallachia and Moldavia were combined to form the United Principalities. Line infantry wore a dark blue single-breasted tunic with red piping. A dark blue kepi with red piping replaced the earlier shako in 1868; a cockade and red pompon were worn on parade. The infantry wore dark grey trousers and had a grey double-breasted greatcoat with collars piped red, spearhead-shaped collar patches and red shoulder straps. Until the late 1860s the Romanian infantry were armed with Dreyse needle-guns. However, during 1867–9 the army acquired 30,000 Peabody rifles from the same company that manufactured the Turkish weapons – the Providence Tool Company of Rhode Island, USA – though not of the same type. The Romanian rifles were built to the original patent of Henry Peabody; they had an external hammer and a slot under the breech block

Close-up of the back sight of the British Snider. Note the Arabic numerals. Sighted to 950 yards, the Snider fired the British
.577 cartridge, with a muzzle velocity of over 1,200 feet per second. (Author's Collection)

opened the action. By 1877 most line infantry regiments, and the chasseur battalion in each division, had Peabody rifles.

H2: Infantryman, Romanian Dorobantzi

The *Dorobantzi* were the infantry of the Romanian territorial army, recruited by conscription and liable for service for a period of eight years. In 1877 the *Dorobantzi* were still armed with obsolete Dreyse needle-guns, which placed them at a grave disadvantage. However, the *Dorobantzi* fought very well, distinguishing themselves in the albeit abortive assault on Plevna. By the autumn their all-white summer uniforms were concealed safely beneath voluminous greatcoats and only their fur caps distinguished them from the regular infantry. Shortly after the war they received the same uniform as the regulars, but with light blue distinctions.

H3: Trooper, Romanian Roshiori

The two regiments of *Roshiori* (regular cavalry) adopted this hussar-style uniform in 1868; the 1st Regiment had yellow bags on the sides of their fur caps, the 2nd white. The eight regiments of *Calarashi* (territorial cavalry) wore dark blue dolmans with red piping and braiding and red bags on their fur caps. The cavalry were organized into three brigades, and often operated in regimental or squadron strength in support of detachments.

Notes sur les planches en couleur

A1 Soldat d'infanterie des lignes russes portant l'uniforme de style 'Pan-Slav' introduce entre 1870 et 1879. La plupart de ces troupes portaient le Krnk 'à trappe' à chargement par la culasse. **A2** Soldat d'infanterie des lignes russes en uniforme d'été blanc, Bulgarie, 1877. La blouse et le [havelock] attachés au képi viennent des guerres d'Asie Centrale. La bayonette fixe était spécifiée par le règlement. **A3** Colonel d'infanterie russe. L'uniforme était similaire à celui des hommes avec l'addition du manteau de 1856, souvent porté comme une cape.

B1 Garde russe en tunique à passepoil blanc et furaska blanche. Il porte un fusil Berdan et a obtenu une bayonette de sapeur de modèle 1834. **B2** Garde russe, janvier 1878, qui porte un manteau marron foncé. Le chiffon entouré autour du mécanisme de son fusil Berden permet d'exclure la neige et la glace. **B3** Cosaque portant le chapeau de fourrure traditionnel. De nombreux cosaques portaient une furashka blanche à la place, mais malgré les tentatives faites pour les organiser ils restèrent surtout une milice tribale.

C1 Les Dragons russes portaient un uniforme similaire à celui de l'infanterie et se battaient souvent à pied. Cependant leur réserve de munitions de 20 cartouches par homme les gênait. **C2** Lieutenant Dubasoff de la Marine russe. Dubasoff est l'un des deux officiers qui menèrent une audacieuse attaque contre les cuirassés turcs sur le Danube. **C3** Tambour de l'infanterie russe, distingué par des ailettes d'épaule.

D1 Canonnier d'artillerie de combat russe en uniforme d'hiver complet, avec des moufles pour protéger ses mains. Sous le manteau il portait une tunique et un pantalon verts. **D2** Général Mikhail Skoboleff, l'officier russe le plus controversé de la guerre, représenté ici à la tête de ses hommes en direction d'une redoute à Plevna. Il s'habillait en blanc et portait un manteau blanc. **D3** Volontaire, Légion bulgare. De nombreux bulgares se joignirent à l'armée russe pour reprendre leur liberté des mains des Turcs. Ils portaient l'uniforme russe et étaient sous la direction d'officiers russes.

E1 Simple soldat turc (nefer) de la Nizamerie active. Le fez rouge était standard, tout comme les vestes et gilets bleus avec passepoil jaune pour le premier régiment de chaque Corps, et rouge pour les autres. La ceinture rouge était un élément non-officiel souvent utilisé. Il est armé d'un fusil Martini-Peabody. **E2** Soldat d'infanterie des bataillons Taillé (Fusiliers). Les Fusiliers portaient des parements verts plutôt que rouges et portaient des bayonnettes-épées plutôt que les bayonnettes triangulaires distribuées à l'infanterie des lignes. **E3** Réserviste turc portant un fusil Snider dépassé.

F1 Soldat d'infanterie turc, uniforme d'hiver, en manteau et bottes improvisées. **F2** Lieutenant-Général Valentine Baka Pasha. Un des nombreux étrangers servant dans l'armée turque. Baker était un ancien officier britannique. Il porte un uniforme de Lieutenant-général turc et a adopté la pratique courante qui consistait à enrouler un turban autour de son fez pour se protéger du soleil. **F3** Un soldat de cavalerie turc. Son uniforme est le même que celui de l'infanterie sauf pour le calot en peau de mouton et les bottes en cuir non tanné. La cavalerie portait l'épée, le révolver et une carabine Winchester de 1873.

G1 Bashi-Bazouk, ou irrégulier turc tribal. **G2** Soldat d'infanterie égyptien. Les troupes égyptiennes qui se battaient avec les turcs étaient organisées selon des principes européens et portaient un uniforme d'hiver bleu foncé. Elles étaient armées de fusils Remington. **G3** Chasseur roumain qui porte l'uniforme inhabituel de ce corps: manteau marron foncé à double boutonnage avec passepoil et parements vert foncé, pantalon gris foncé et chapeau de cuir noir. Pour la grande tenue le chapeau était agrémenté d'une plume de coq verte et de la cocarde roumaine. Le matériel était noir et le fusil était un Peabody.

H1 Soldat d'infanterie roumain en tunique et képi bleu foncé, avec passepoil rouge, et pantalon gris. L'infanterie portait un manteau gris à double boutonnage avec un passepoil rouge sur le col, des écussons de col et des bretelles d'épaule. La plupart des troupes roumaines étient armées de fusils Peabody américains de type différent de celui porté par les turcs. **H2** Soldat d'infanterie des Dorobantzi, l'armée territoriale roumaine. Ils portaient un uniforme d'été blanc, souvent caché par un manteau, et des calots de fourrure. Ils étaient armés de fusils obsolètes Dreyse à aiguille. **H3** Soldat de cavalerie des deux régiments Roshiori (cavalerie régulière), portant l'uniforme de style Hussard adopté en 1868. Le 1er Régiment avait des sacs jaunes sur le côté du calot de fourrure et pour le 2nd ils étaient blancs. Let huit régiments de Calarashi, ou cavalerie territoriale, portaient un dolman bleu foncé avec un passepoil rouge et avaient des sacs rouges sur le calot.

Farbtafeln

A1 Russischer Front-Infanterist in der Uniform 'panslawishen' Stils, die in den 70er Jahren des 19. Jahrhunderts eingeführt wurde. Die meisten dieser Truppen hatten den 'Klappen'–Hinterlader Krnk. **A2** Russischer Front-Infanterist in der weißen Sommeruniform, Bulgarien 1877. Sowohl die Uniformjacke als auch der am Kappi befestigte Nackenschurz stammen aus den Kriegen in Zentralasien; das feste Bajonett war amtlich vorgeschrieben. **A3** Oberst der russischen Infanterie. Die Uniform war der der Soldaten ähnlich und hatte zusätzlich einen 1856er Überzieher, der oft wie ein Umhang getragen wurde.

B1 Russischer Gardesoldat in weiß paspelierter Tunika und weißer *Furashka*. Er trägt ein Berdan-Gewehr und hat sich ein Sappeur-Bajonett Modell 1834 angeschafft. **B2** Russischer Gardesoldat, Januar 1878, in erdbraunem Überzieher. Das Tuch, das um den Mechanismus seines Berdan-Gewehrs gewickelt ist, soll es vor Schnee und Eis schützen. **B3** Kosak mit der traditionellen Pelzmütze. Viele Kosaken trugen stattdessen weiße *Furashkas*, doch trotz eingehender Versuche, sie zu organisieren, blieben sie dem Wesen nach doch eine Stammesmiliz.

C1 Doe russischen Dragoner trugen eine der Infanterie ähnliche Uniform und kämpften oft zu Fuß, obgleich sie durch die Munitionsration von 20 Runden pro Mann eingeschränkt waren. **C2** Leutnant Dubasoff von der russischen Marine. Dubasoff war einer der zwei Offiziere, die eine gewagte Attacke auf die türkischen Panzerschiffe auf der Donau anführten. **C3** Russischer Infanterie-Trommler, an den Schulterabzeichen erkenntlich.

D1 Kanonier der russischen Feldartillerie in kompletter Winterausrüstung mit Fäustlingen, die seine Hände vor der Kälte schützen. Unter dem Überzieher trägt er eine grüne Tunika und Hosen. **D2** General Mikhail Skoboleff, der umstrittenste russische Offizier des Krieges, ist hier abgebildet, wie er seine Männer in eine Redoute in Plevna führt. Er trug weiß und einen weißen Mantel. **D3** Freiwilliger, Bulgarische Legion. Viele Bulgaren schlossen sich der russischen Armee an, um Freiheit von den Türken zu erringen; sie trugen russische Uniformen und unterstanden russischen Offizieren.

E1 Türkischer gemeiner Berufssoldat (*Nefer*) der aktiven *Nizamerie*. Der rote Fes gehörte zur Standardausrüstung, wie auch die blauen Jacken und Westen, die beim ersten Regiment eines jeden Korps gelb paspeliert waren, bei den übrigen rot. Die rote Schärpe war ein beliebter inoffizieller Zusatz; er ist mit einem Martini-Peabody-Gewehr bewaffnet. **E2** Infanterist der *Taillé* (Schützen)-Bataillons. Die Schutzenbrigade hatte grüne Aufschläge anstelle der roten und Schwertbajonette anstelle der dreieckigen, die an die Frontinfanterie ausgegeben wurden. **E3** Türkischer Reservist in der neu ausgegebenen Standard-Infanterieuniform, jedoch mit einem überholten Snider-Gewehr.

F1 Türkischer Infanterist in der Winteruniform mit Überzieher und improvisierten Stiefeln. **F2** Generalleutnant Valentine Baker Pasha. Baker war einer mehrerer Ausländer, die in der türkischen Armee dienten, und war ein ehemaliger britischer Offizier; er trägt die Uniform eines türkischen Generalleutnants und folgt dem weit verbreiteten Usus, als Sonnenschutz einen Turban um seinen Fes zu wickeln **F3** Türkischer Berufskavallerist. Seine Uniform ist bis auf die Schaffellmütze und die ungegerbten Lederstiefel mit der der Infanterie identisch. Die Kavallerie war mit Schwertern, Revolvern und Winchester-Karabinern des Modells 1873 bewaffnet.

G1 *Bashi-Bazouk*, beziehungsweise türkischer Stammesfreischärler. **G2** Ägyptischer Infanterist. Die ägyptischen Truppen, die mit den Türken kämpften, waren nach europäischem Muster organisiert und trugen dunkelblaue Winteruniformen. Sie waren mit Remington-Gewehren bewaffnet. **G3** Rumänischer *Chasseur* in der ungewöhnlichen Uniform, die aus einem dunkelbraunen, zweireihigen Mantel mit grünen Paspeln und Aufschlägen bestand, dunkelgrauen Hosen und einem schwarzen Lederhut. Bei der Paradeuniform war der Hut mit einer grünen Hahnenfeder auf der und der rumänischen Kokarde geschmückt. Ihre Ausrüstung war schwarz und sie waren mit Peabody-Gewehren bewaffnet.

H1 Rumänischer Frontinfanterist in dunkelblauer Tunika und Käppit mit roten Paspeln und grauen Hosen. Die Infanterie trug einen grauen, zweireihigen Überzieher mit roten Paspeln am Kragen, Kragenstücken und Schulterklappen. Die meisten rumänischen Truppen waren mit amerikanischen Peabody-Gewehren bewaffnet, und zwar von einem anderen Typ, als ihn die Türken hatten. **H2** Infanterist der *Dorobantzi*, der rumänischen Territorialarmee. Sie trug weiße Sommeruniformen, die gewöhnlich von einem Überzieher verdeckt wurden, und Pelzmützen. Sie war mit überholten Dreyse-Zündnadelgewehren bewaffnet. **H3** Kavallerist der beiden *Roshiori* (Berufskavallerie)-Regimenter in der husarenartigen Uniform, die 1868 übernommen wurde. Das 1. Regiment hatte gelbe Taschen an den Seiten der Pelzmütze, das 2. weiße. Die acht Regimenter der *Calarashi*, der Territorialkavallerie, trug dunkelblaue Dolmane mit roten Paspeln und hatte rote Taschen an den Mützen.